GOD'S CREATURES
A Biblical View of Animals

GOD'S CREATURES
A Biblical View of Animals

Susan Bulanda

CLADACH
Publishing

Copyright © 2008
by Susan Bulanda
All rights reserved
Printed in the U.S.A.

Published by CLADACH Publishing
Greeley, Colorado
www.cladach.com

ISBN: 9780975961988
Library of Congress Control Number: 2008923293

Cover design by Deanna Boveé
Front cover photo credit: iStockphoto
Back cover photos by: Chris and Mira Jones (donkeys),
Alisann Crough (superb starling), C. Lawton (coyote)

Scripture quotations, unless otherwise noted, are from the
New American Standard Bible®.

Bible quotes taken with permission from The Ryrie Study
Bible, Moody Publishers, © 1995 updated by Charles
C. Ryrie; the New American Standard Bible® (NASB),
Copyright © 1975 by the Lockman Foundation; The
Amplified® Bible (AMP), Copyright © 1987 by the
Lockman Foundation and Zondervan Publishing House;
the New Revised Standard Version ® (NRSV), Copyright
©1989 by the National Council of the Churches of Christ
in the United States of America.

To my son Thomas, USMC, and to all the men and women who serve and have served in our armed forces: Thank you.

CONTENTS

INTRODUCTION

ALL MY LIFE I have been involved with animals, mostly dogs, cats and horses. One of my earliest pets was a cat named Puff. I named her after the cat in the *Dick, Jane and Sally* reader series. Puff and I grew up together and I was a young adult when she died at age thirteen. I assumed that she went to heaven.

As I grew in my Christian faith, however, I heard many different opinions about whether or not animals will be in heaven. It seemed as though no one knew for certain; they merely made assumptions based on what they heard or read. Some religious leaders simply did not think that the matter was important or worthy of consideration.

Now, as a dog trainer and an animal behavior consultant I am often called to help people cope with the loss of their beloved pets. I am frequently asked whether or not animals will be in heaven. As my clients look to me for answers, I have come to realize this is an important issue to many people.

This book is a result of my quest for answers. I will share with you what the Bible teaches about animals; how animals have a special place in the Scriptures; and how God uses them to teach us some important lessons.

Do not look at the material in this book with second-hand information about the Bible. Do not believe rumors or other people's opinions about what the Bible says. Go to the source. If you have never read the Bible, I urge you to do so.

I have met people whose belief that Christian theology

excludes animals from heaven caused them to lose their faith in God. How could God ignore this wonderful part of his creation, they ask. It may help to remind these people that what is implied in the Bible about animals is important, as well as what is stated explicitly. Although animals are not the main focus of the Bible, they are a big part of God's created world and have a special place in his Word. However I want to make it clear that in no way do I mean to say or imply that animals are equal to or better than humans. Animals are part of the plan and will of God, just like all the rest of his creation.

Please, open your mind, ask questions, seek answers, and explore the information in this book. But more importantly, read your Bible. Do not take what I say at face value; learn for yourself. In *Christianity and the Rights of Animals*, Andrew Linzey (who is both a chaplain and an animal lover) states, "Christian theology provides some of the best arguments for respecting animal life and for taking seriously animals as partners with us within God's creation." Linzey also points out that, though he has researched Christianity and animals, he has found no major study devoted to this topic. In his opinion the theological significance of animals has yet to be explored. Linzey writes, "We have to face the fact that when it comes to determining Jesus' actual attitude to animals, in the records as we now have them at least, we have to work largely from hints and guesses. But these are on the whole certainly more positive than negative."

This book will help you develop a better understanding of the nature and mind of animals, according to Scripture and recent scientific research. May you be encouraged and blessed as you read.

1
CREATED WILD AND DOMESTIC

As I GAZE into the eyes of my beloved pets, both dogs and cats, I have often wondered about the depths of their feelings, what their thoughts are. Is there more to the relationship between humans and animals than is obvious? All through my life, my animals have been there to share my sorrows and my joys. I think God must have had good reasons for making them the way he did.

One time as a young girl I buried my face in my cat Puff's fur while I cried over some now-forgotten incident. I remember the connection that I felt, the comfort that she gave me when I needed it—how she gently licked the tears from my cheeks and tried to cheer me with her purring.

Did God create animals to be helpers for us in ways that we don't understand?

The book of Genesis provides the foundation for understanding the role of animals, in our lives as well as in God's overall plan. Therefore we will start in the very beginning with the act of creation and the events which took place in the Garden of Eden. Here are revealed some of the answers to the mysteries that surround our relationship with animals.

First let us look at the creation story as recorded in the Bible:

And God said, 'Let the waters bring forth swarms of

living creatures, and let birds fly above the earth across
the dome of the sky.' So God created the great sea mon-
sters and every living creature that moves, with which the
waters swarm, according to their kinds, and every winged
bird of every kind. And God saw that it was good. God
blessed them, saying, 'Be fruitful and multiply and fill the
waters in the seas, and let birds multiply on the earth.'
And there was evening and there was morning, the fifth
day.

And God said, 'Let the earth bring forth living creatures of every kind: cattle and creeping things and wild
animals of the earth of every kind.' And it was so. God
made the wild animals of the earth of every kind, and
the cattle of every kind, and everything that creeps upon
the ground of every kind. And God saw that it was good.
(Gen. 1:20-25 NRSV)

Notice the Bible makes a clear distinction between wild and
domestic animals. Although humans may tame a wild animal,
they may never make it domestic; a domestic animal has an
entirely different role to play. God created animals for specific
purposes. Some of those purposes are obvious, some are not. This
raises questions about whether or not some animals descended
from others, such as the dog from the wolf, as has been believed.

Genesis tells us that humans, not animals, were made in
the image of God. Although only humans were made in God's
image, he loves the wild and domestic animals so much that he
uses them, along with humankind, to accomplish his purposes.

Often when we read the Bible, we only study the relationship
between people and God, sin and salvation. While this is the
main focus of the Bible, there are also many more subtle aspects
of life on earth that the Bible can teach us. God created this earth

and all that is in it, for two purposes: first, for his own pleasure, and second, to support humans. God and his angels did not need the earthly world. They were doing just fine in heaven.

We see that God had a specific order to his creation. First he created the heavens as we know them. Next he created the earth as we know it, with land, water, air, day, and night. The air, earth and water are necessary to support vegetation. So next God created the vegetation needed to support other kinds of life. After that he created the stars, sun and moon. At this point, all the earthly and heavenly systems were in place to support all life.

Next God created the creatures of the sea and the air. After that he created land animals, cattle and creeping things. Even before humans were created, God makes a distinction between wild and domestic animals (verse 25). "Cattle" refer to all domestic animals, and "wild animals" is sometimes translated "beasts."

This is not the only place in the Bible where there is a distinction made between wild animals and domestic animals. Today we know that certain kinds of animals live well with people and others do not. Although some wild animals can be tamed, they are never really domesticated. Circus animals are good examples of this. Although the big cats can be taught to perform, they are never fully trustworthy because they are not domesticated. They do not have the total willingness to work and live with humans and cannot be trusted not to harm them.

Another example of this is the peculiar situation that exists in the United States regarding tigers. According to the Animal Centers of Excellence, there are three times more captive, backyard bred[1] tigers in the United States than there are in the wild. People purchase the cubs hoping to make them pets. However, they are finding that tigers, even after generations of captive backyard breeding, cannot be completely domesticated and may still attack their owners without warning.

Monkeys are another example of wild animals who resist domestication. Attempts to teach monkeys to be service animals for the handicapped have been unsuccessful. In 2005 a California man visiting a chimpanzee in a rescue facility for monkeys that can no longer be kept as pets was attacked and mutilated by two male chimps. While the one he himself had raised was not one of the two which attacked him, the man had had to give up his chimp in the first place because the animal was prone to acts of violence; it had injured a police officer and bitten a woman's finger.

The Animal Protection Institute's list of primate attacks shows that all types of pet monkeys will attack their owners. The list comprises only those incidents which have been reported; it may be inferred that there are many more which have not been acknowledged.

Still another reference to our inability to tame certain types of animals is found in an article by Jared Diamond, "The Shape of Africa," published in the September 2005 *National Geographic*:

> The domesticated sheep and cattle for Fertile Crescent origins took about 5,000 years to spread from the Mediterranean down to the southern tip of Africa. The continent's own native animals—with the exception of guinea fowl and possibly donkeys and one breed of cattle—proved impossible to domesticate.

Researchers continue to raise questions about the origin of animals and how some animals, such as dogs, became companions to humans. The most recent evidence supports the distinction made in the Bible, that certain animals were created wild and others domesticated.

An example of this shift in thinking is found in an article

in the *Smithsonian*, March 1999 titled, "Tracking America's First Dog" by Scott Weidensaul. In it, the author explores the origins of the Carolina dog. It is believed that the Carolina dog, found in the rural areas of South Carolina, may be what is left of the original dogs that crossed the Bering land bridge into North America. These dogs appear in paintings of Native Americans. Weidensaul reports in his article that in 1997 a team of evolutionary biologists studied the DNA of wild canids and wolves and decided that there was a split between dogs and wolves before anyone suspected that domestication was possible.

The article quotes archaeozoologist Susan Crockford as saying that the standard explanation of domestication—bringing young wild animals into the home, taming and breeding them to create domesticated animals—is a myth. Weidensaul goes on to say that "Whether you're talking about dogs, sheep, cows, goats, pigs or water buffalo, there are consistent differences between the wild and domesticated forms."

In a related study, Dr. Gustavo Aguirre, at Cornell University's Institute for Animal Health, found that dogs' mitochondria DNA (mtDNA) reveal that they split off from wolves about 130,000 years ago, long before they were domesticated by man.

The Bible tells us what God did when he created animals, but does not give us all the details. The latest research suggests that the commonly-held belief that humans interacted with the friendliest wild animals and then bred them to be the domestic animals of today seems to be inaccurate.[2]

Note that the Bible's creation account states more than once that each animal was made according to its kind, or "of every kind," each distinct and separate, not from another earlier animal as evolutionists would have us believe.

But just what does "kind" mean? Dr. Charles C. Ryrie, a well-known scholar and theologian, comments,

There are fixed boundaries beyond which reproductive variations cannot go, but it is impossible to know whether 'kind' is to be equated with families, genera, or some other category of biological classification.

After God created all the earth, its vegetation, animals and creatures, he said it was good. He also blessed all creatures, telling them to be fruitful and multiply.[3]

Humans were the last beings that God created. This is not because humans are less valuable than the rest of creation, but because all things were finally prepared for humans. The Bible does make it clear that the animals of earth were made from the same material as humans.

Then the Lord God formed man from the dust of the ground and breathed into his nostrils the breath or spirit of life, and man became a living being. . . . Out of the ground the Lord God formed every beast of the field and every bird of the sky. (Gen. 2:7, 19 AMP)

In this case, the breath or spirit of life refers to the whole spiritual being of humans, the soul and spirit. In the Ryrie Study Bible, Dr. Ryrie has this to say in his notes for Genesis 2:7:

Man's body was formed from small particles of the earth (the Hebrew words for man and earth are similar; cf. 1 Cor. 15:47), but his life came from the breath of God. *A living being*, i.e., a living person. The phrase is also used of animals (1:21, 24). Man is distinguished from animals by being created in the image of God.

Humans were created in a natural and moral likeness to God.

Then God said, 'Let Us[4] make man in Our image,
according to Our likeness; and let them rule over the fish
of the sea and over the birds of the sky and over the cattle
and over all the earth, and over every creeping thing that
creeps on the earth.' (Gen. 1:26)

The natural likeness refers to a human's intellectual and
emotional make-up, which is similar to that of God. Also, a
human's right to rule is assigned by God. When Adam and Eve
sinned, they lost their moral aspect but retained their natural
resemblance to God. This of course was passed on and applies to
the whole human race.

Another major difference between humans and animals is
that God breathed the spirit of life into humans, which includes
the soul. While God certainly created all of the animals alive,
humans received a soul which animals did not receive.[5] For a
more detailed explanation of the difference between spirit and
soul see chapter 14, "Will Animals Go to heaven?"

So we see that all of creation—earth, sun, stars, air, plants,
animals, everything—was created for the glory and pleasure of
God. It was also created to benefit humans, both for our enjoyment and our survival.

The order of events was as follows:

1. God created the earth.
2. He created the environment to support life.
3. He created the plants and animals on the earth.
4. He created humans.

Everything was created to support humans—not only to
provide them with shelter and food, but to provide physical,
aesthetic pleasure and comfort. As we learn more about the

interdependency of all earth's inhabitants, we get a glimpse of the immensity and intricacy of God's creation. We clearly see that it is beyond our human ability to fully understand and comprehend.

2
ADAM & THE ANIMALS

ANIMALS HAVE A WAY of bringing people together. How many times have we heard stories about two people who meet because of an animal? Often a wonderful relationship grows from this meeting: a friendship, or even a marriage. Over the years I have made life-long friends because they came to me to have their dog trained or because they had a problem with their cat. I have also met some of my most valued friends at animal conferences. Many times as I have been out walking my dog, people who are normally reserved have stopped to talk to me. I have done the same. It has always amazed me how friendly total strangers can be when they stop to talk about an animal.

God has been using animals since the Garden of Eden to help people with their relationships with each other. In a sense, animals helped bring Adam and Eve together. Let's see how God used animals to help Adam understand his need for Eve.

In order to fully appreciate the role animals played in this event, try to imagine Adam in the Garden of Eden without Eve. Adam's job in Eden was to tend the garden, eat the fruit, and name the animals. He enjoyed the company of God each evening and had no sin in his heart or life. This meant that he had no problems, was never sick, did not need money, liked his job, and had the best friend anyone could have—God himself. It is reasonable to assume that he was content with life. But God knew that Adam needed the companionship of another human

being, even if Adam did not fully recognize his own need.
God created in Adam the desire for human companionship.
How could God show Adam, in the perfect environment of the
Garden, that he needed something more?

> Then the LORD God said, 'It is not good that the man
> should be alone; I will make him a helper as his partner.'
> So out of the ground the Lord God formed every animal
> of the field and every bird of the air, and brought them
> to the man to see what he would call them; and whatever
> the man called every living creature, that was its name.
> The man gave names to all cattle, and to the birds of the
> air, and to every animal of the field; but for the man there
> was not found a helper for his partner. (Gen. 2:18-20
> NRSV)

I see five reasons why God had Adam name all the animals.
First, God directed Adam to compare himself to all of the
animals and seek a being to complement him; in doing so, Adam
realized that he was the only human on the earth. There was
no suitable helper for him in the animal kingdom. Second, when
God created Eve, Adam then realized that she was just like him
and very special. Third, God gave Adam the authority to name
the animals, showing Adam and the animals that humankind had
authority over the rest of the earth. Fourth, it showed that the
animals were special to God. They were important enough to be
given names. Fifth, God used animals to teach Adam.

Because Adam was the first created human, he had no prior
family life. His only family was God. Adam saw, from his first
day on earth, animals interacting as families. The animals were
not afraid of him; he saw the young playing, and the tenderness
of the adults toward the young. God may have wanted to further

show Adam an example of family life when he had Adam pay close attention to the animals while he named them. Perhaps God used the animals to plant the first seeds of what relationships and family life are all about.

We see that God used animals to teach Adam a number of important lessons. Adam learned that he had dominion over the animals; he saw the dynamics of family relationships, tenderness toward the young, and love of a mate; he saw that he was unique in the world and thus very special; he saw how special Eve was; and he saw God's love for his creation.

It is fun to think of Adam telling Eve about his experiences, showing her all of the plants and animals in the Garden, and sharing his animal companions with her.

As animal lovers we can only dream about life where animals have no fear of humans. But we can appreciate the lessons that Adam and Eve learned from their animal friends.

3
GOD CARES FOR ANIMALS

As we consider all of the cruelty in the world that is directed at animals, we have to wonder: If God cares about animals, why would he allow this to happen? Animals are innocent victims that did nothing to deserve the bad things that happen to them.

The Bible tells us that God loves all his creation very much.

> For God so loved *the world* that He gave His only begotten Son, that whoever believes in Him shall not perish, but have eternal life. For God did not send the Son into the world to judge the world, but that *the world* might be saved through Him. (John 3:16-17, emphasis added)

Note that these are the words of Jesus, and he says "the world," not just humans. The term used in the Greek is *kosmos*, which is commonly used to mean the universe. Jesus died to save humans, and in doing so, saved all his creation as well. Jesus died specifically for all people because humans sinned. Since the entire creation suffers from the sin of humans, God's plan of salvation is all-inclusive. We know this because the Bible tells us that all of creation will be freed from the bondage of sin when Jesus rules the world.

Despite the fact that none of the animals sinned, the behavior of the people who own animals will often cause God's punishment or blessing to include animals, and in some cases the land as well.

The Bible gives us many examples of God's love for his earthly creatures. The first and most obvious: he created them. After he created them he blessed them, and said his creation was very good. When he sent the Flood, he purposely saved representatives of all the creatures. He could have easily created new animals, but he chose to save the ones that he had already made.

Also, while God gave Noah and his family permission to use animals as food after the Flood, he put the fear of humans into the animals to protect them and give them a chance to survive. This inborn fear of humans is evident in domesticated animals that have not been raised by humans. The kittens born to a domestic cat in the wild are fearful of people, even if their mother will allow people to feed and pet her. Yet still, with patience, the kittens may be trained to lose their fear. If the animal comes from a domestic species, people can work with the animal to overcome the fear of humans; but if the animal comes from a wild species, there is never a solid transition.

After the Flood, before he put the fear of humans into the animals, God made a covenant with them. Imagine Noah, his family and all of the creatures from the ark gathered together as God spoke to them.

'As for me, I am establishing my covenant with you and your descendants after you, and with every living creature that is with you, the birds, the domestic animals, and every animal of the earth with you, as many as came out of the ark. I establish my covenant with you, that never again shall all flesh be cut off by the waters of a flood, and never again shall there be a flood to destroy the earth.' God said, 'This is the sign of the covenant that I make between me and you and every living creature that is with you, for all future generations; I have set my bow in the clouds, and it shall be a sign of the covenant between me and the earth. When I bring clouds over the earth and the bow is seen in the clouds, I will remember my covenant that is between me and you and every living creature of all flesh; and the waters shall never again become a flood to destroy all flesh. When the bow is in the clouds, I will see it and remember the everlasting covenant between God and every living creature of all flesh that is on the earth.' (Gen. 9:9-17 NRSV)

Notice that God specifically mentions the animals, or "every living creature." And he names them by groups—"birds," "domestic animals," and "every animal of the earth" (all wild creatures). To speak of them this way, he must care for them.

Another example of God's concern is found in the portion of Mosaic law relating to food for working animals:

You should not muzzle an ox when it treads out the grain. (Deut. 25:4)

In other words, if the animal works for us, we are responsible for feeding it and caring for it.

Although this passage is expanded upon in the New Testament (1 Timothy 5:18 and 1 Corinthians 9:9) to illustrate that a person should receive fair wages for his work, it also shows that God values kindness to the animals that labor for humans. The Apostle Paul pointed out that God cares about the animals he created, but cares more about humans.

Proverbs makes it very clear that God considers it a sign of righteousness to show kindness to animals:

A righteous man has regard for the life of his beast, but the compassion of the wicked is cruel. (Prov. 12:10)

This passage also teaches us that the way we treat animals is an indication of our character. Most adults who show cruelty or violence toward other people, were abusive to animals when they were young. This fact has been established by the Humane Society of the United States. Psychologists and law enforcement officers also recognize the significance of animal cruelty behavior in children and adults. Measuring acts of cruelty to animals has been part of the criteria used by psychologists in studying and understanding conduct disorders. It is interesting that the Bible indicated this thousands of years ago.

It is important to demonstrate and teach our children and grandchildren kindness to animals.

Now consider this passage:

If you meet your enemy's ox or his donkey wandering away, you shall surely return it to him. If you see the donkey of one who hates you lying helpless under its load, you shall refrain from leaving it to him, you shall surely release it with him. . . . You shall sow your land for six years and gather in its yield, but on the seventh year you shall let it rest and lie fallow, so that the needy of your people may eat; and whatever they leave the beast of the field may eat. You are to do the same with your vineyard and your olive grove. Six days you are to do your work, but on the seventh day you shall cease from labor in order that your ox and your donkey may rest, and the son of your female slave, as well as your stranger, may refresh themselves. (Ex. 23:4, 11-12)

Here God has made provisions for the animals as well as for humans. The animals are to be allowed to rest on the seventh day of the week, and in the seventh year the wild animals are allowed to eat from the fields. If one sees an ox or donkey overloaded, even if one does not like the animal's owner, God commands that the person help the animal. This law is also for the benefit of humans, since an act of kindness toward the animal could help to mend a strained relationship between two people. God further commands in Deuteronomy 22:1-2 that if a person finds an animal and does not know to whom it belongs, he must keep the animal and care for it until the owner claims it. Again, this benefits both the owner and the animal; the animal is fed, housed and protected from predators, and the owner has a chance to recover his animal.

Repeatedly in the Bible, God claims all of creation as his own. In Psalm 50, for example, the psalmist explains that God does not need animal sacrifices because all the animals are his anyway.

I do not reprove you for your sacrifices,
And your burnt offerings are continually before Me.
I shall take no young bull out of your house
Nor male goats out of your folds.
For every beast of the forest is Mine,
The cattle on a thousand hills.
I know all the birds of the mountains,
And everything that moves in the field is Mine.
(Ps. 50:8-11)

In Psalm 104 the psalmist points out that God made the earth with the needs of the animals and people in mind, and God cares and provides for his creatures:

You make springs gush forth in the valleys; they flow
between the hills, giving drink to every wild animal;
the wild asses quench their thirst. By the streams the
birds of the air have their habitation; they sing among
the branches. From your lofty abode you water the
mountains; the earth is satisfied with the fruit of your
work. You cause the grass to grow for the cattle, and
plants for people to use, to bring forth food from the
earth, and wine to gladden the human heart, oil to make
the face shine, and bread to strengthen the human heart.
The trees of the LORD are watered abundantly, the cedars
of Lebanon that he planted. In them the birds build their
nests; the stork has its home in the fir trees. The high
mountains are for the wild goats; the rocks are a refuge
for the coneys. (Ps. 104:10-18 NRSV)

When God reprimanded Jonah for questioning his desire to
save the city of Nineveh, he expressly included the animals of
Nineveh among those who would suffer if the people in the city
did not change their ways.

And should I not be concerned about Nineveh, that
great city in which there are more than a hundred and
twenty thousand persons who do not know their right
hand from their left, and also many animals? (Jonah 4:11
NRSV)

God did not need to mention the animals to make his point
about the city. But by mentioning them, he illustrates his care for
the creatures that would otherwise suffer from the punishment
to come.

Jesus explains in the Gospel of Matthew that God takes care

of those who work and have faith. He uses the birds and animals as an example to show us that as much as God cares for animals, he cares more for people.

> Look at the birds of the air; they neither sow nor reap nor gather into barns, and yet your heavenly Father feeds them. (Matt. 6:26 NRSV)

This passage does not mean that the birds and animals do not work. As we know from studies of nature, all things have a purpose and a job to do. However, they do not plant to produce food; God provides the food for the birds and animals. But the birds and animals must work to gather the food.

God gives another example that he cares for animals and people:

> Are not two sparrows sold for a penny? Yet not one of them will fall to the ground apart from your Father. . . . Are not five sparrows sold for two pennies? Yet not one of them is forgotten in God's sight. . . . Consider the ravens: they neither sow nor reap, they have neither storehouse nor barn, and yet God feeds them. Of how much more value are you than the birds! (Matt. 10:29; Luke 12:6 & 24 NRSV)

The price of a penny shows that the sparrows had little worth to humans, yet God knows exactly what happens to them.

The Bible gives us many examples of God's love for all of his creation, including the animals that he created. God did not make anything that he does not love or care about.

Is it possible that in modern times, God has put the desire to care for all animals in the hearts of many people? When we think of all the animal trainers, humane volunteers, people who use animals for therapy purposes and so forth, it is not hard to imagine that the love of animals and the desire to care for them is God's love for his creation showing through humans. If we add all of the people who care for and love plants, we see an army of people who care for God's creation.

4
THE KILLING & THE EATING OF ANIMALS

KILLING ANIMALS

The thought of killing animals is repulsive to many people. If God loves all of his creation, why would he allow the death of animals? Why would he make an animal bear the first death in the history of humankind? These are some of the vexing questions that animal lovers face. But a closer look at the book of Genesis gives us an explanation. In the account of the Fall of Man, when Adam and Eve ate from the tree which God told them not to touch, we read:

> 'From any tree of the garden you may eat freely; but from the tree of the knowledge of good and evil you shall not eat, for in the day that you eat from it you shall surely die.' (Gen. 2:16-17)

When Adam and Eve ate from the forbidden tree, their eyes were opened and they realized that they were naked. They made aprons of fig leaves to cover themselves. When they heard God walking in the garden they hid because they knew that they had disobeyed God and were fearful and ashamed (*See* Gen. 3:7-8).

The aprons of leaves were meant to cover their physical nakedness, but on a deeper level Adam and Eve were trying to cover or fix their own sins. Their intimate relationship with God was broken. When the evening came, the time when they usually walked with God, they were hiding, afraid to face him. But God called to them, asking where they were, even though he knew very well where they were and what they had done. He knew that Adam and Eve did not fully understand what had taken place. So after they responded to him, he had them first give an account of what they had done; then he explained to them the gravity of their sin.

God showed them that although they would not experience immediate physical death, still death had now entered the world. Their spiritual death, the death of their soul, occurred immediately, and could not be fixed by them alone. Their physical death would follow, something that they did not understand because up until that point there had been no death in the world.

After Adam and Eve confessed what they had done, God reprimanded them, and then cursed—along with all creation— the serpent who had tempted them to sin. Next God showed Adam and Eve what physical death meant. He killed an animal and then,

> The Lord God made garments of skin for Adam and his wife, and clothed them. (Gen. 3:21)

By making clothes of skin, God not only showed them the nature of physical death, but more importantly, that humans could not fix their own sins. Only God could do that. The killing of an animal showed humans that the shedding of blood in a sacrifice of death was necessary to cancel out their sin. The animal that was killed was guiltless and innocent, foreshadowing the future sacrifice on the cross of Jesus Christ, who would be innocent and guiltless as well.

The sacrifice in the Garden of Eden began the practice of

animal sacrifice to atone for human sin, which lasted until Jesus came. Once Jesus died, animal sacrifice was no longer necessary. Jesus was the ultimate sacrifice that took away the sin of the world.

In the sacrifice of that first animal to make physical coverings for Adam and Eve, God gave humankind their first symbolic promise of redemption from sin. He provided a way to escape spiritual death, and he used an animal to do it. In that respect, God has given animals a special honor, a special job.

He gave animals a very important part to play in the lesson about the salvation of humans. Animal sacrifice in the Old Testament was the constant reminder of a Savior to come. The sacrificial animal—which had to be an animal without blemish (*See* Numbers 19:1)—was a symbol of Jesus on the cross.

Jesus obeyed the will of his father concerning the salvation of humans. Animals also did the will of God and of their earthly owners. They walked meekly to the slaughter, just as Jesus did. They died for something that was not their fault. They shed their blood, just as Jesus did.

In no way were these animals elevated to the status of the Messiah. They were merely a symbol of the coming Savior to the Old Testament believers. Unlike Jesus, no animal has risen from the grave or performed miracles. But Satan, in his usual way of twisting the truth, has influenced many civilizations to worship animals and animal-like idols instead of God. This is one of the ways Satan has tried to discredit, distort, and twist the message of God. However, the very fact that Satan has used animals for his evil purposes echoes the importance of animal sacrifice in the Old Testament.

Some people may think that God likes to destroy animals by using them in a ritual sacrifice. However, a close study of Old Testament sacrifices and New Testament texts on the subject reveal otherwise.

'Sacrifices and offerings and whole burnt offerings and
sacrifices for sin You have not desired, nor have You taken
pleasure in them' (which are offered according to the
Law). Then He said, 'Behold I have come to do Your will.'
He takes away the first in order to establish the second. By
this will we have been sanctified through the offering of
the body of Jesus Christ once for all. (Heb. 10: 8-10)

This states that God the Father never enjoyed animal sacrifice. It was done for humans, to give people a way to atone for, or
cover their sins for one year. The Day of Atonement is observed
once a year under Mosaic law; it was meant to remind people
that they are sinners. The sacrifice never actually took away the
sin, only covered it.

Yet in those sacrifices there is a reminder of sins year by
year. For it is impossible for the blood of bulls and goats
to take away sin. (Heb. 10:3-4)

Only Jesus could take away the sins of humans. It took his
death and resurrection to do this; absolutely nothing else would
work. The practice of animal sacrifice was for humans, not to
satisfy or appease God.

When Jesus died as a sacrifice, he ended the old (the first)
practice of animal sacrifice, since Jesus' sacrifice (the second) was
complete and fulfilled prophesy.

So an animal was killed in the Garden of Eden to show
Adam and Eve in what manner God would fix their sins. This
was a lesson for the people yet to come. Nothing humans could
do was or is able to take away the sin that Adam and Eve com-
mitted, or our own sins. By sacrificing an animal, God gave his
first promise of future redemption. God laid out the conditions.

Blood had to be shed—the blood of an innocent, sinless being. Because only humans sinned, a human had to die. Because no human was or is sinless, God had to provide his own sacrifice. We are given another glimpse of this in the story of Abraham and Isaac recounted in Genesis 22. God decided to test Abraham's obedience; he told Abraham to kill his only son Isaac and sacrifice him in the same way that animals were sacrificed. In strict obedience to God, Abraham prepared to do this. When the boy Isaac asked Abraham where the sacrificial animal was (he saw that they were going to offer a sacrifice to God and did not have an animal), Abraham told Isaac that God would provide the sacrifice.

When it came time, Abraham tied up his son and got ready to kill him. However, an angel of the Lord stopped Abraham and told him not to kill Isaac.

Then Abraham raised his eyes and looked, and behold, behind him a ram caught in the thicket by his horns. (Gen. 22:13)

We know that this was a miracle because the words "and behold" indicate that Abraham was surprised and that the ram had not been there a few minutes before.

This foreshadows the offering of God's own Son Jesus, who was both man and God, as a sacrifice. The first physical death of an animal in Eden presaged a Redeemer to come; it demonstrated to all people that they could not fix their own sins, but that it had to be done through the grace of God.

Andrew Linzey offers an additional view of animal sacrifice in his discussion of the difference between the death of an animal and the offering of lifeblood. According to Linzey, true animal sacrifice was the offering of lifeblood.

But what did it mean to offer lifeblood (*nephesh*) to the Creator? First of all, it meant that all life was a gift from God and therefore belonged to him. Secondly, the act of returning to the Creator was probably understood (by those who practiced it) as the offering of life. Thirdly, and perhaps most importantly, the practice of sacrifice thereby assumed that the life of the individual animal continued beyond mortal death. In these ways it is possible to understand the historic practice of sacrifice as affirming the value of the animals slain and not simply as their gratuitous destruction. The tradition of sacrifice did not necessarily involve a low view of animal life. (pg. 41)

Interestingly, this view seems to assume that the animal has a life after death.

Since the Fall in the Garden of Eden, the only way a person can return to God is by accepting his plan of salvation and eternal life.

In this plan, after a physical death, the saved person returns to the presence of God. So Linzey's ideas regarding animal sacrifice are in line with the plan of human salvation.

We see that an animal had to die in the Garden of Eden as a promise to humans that God would provide a way for salvation. Animals suffer from the effects of our sin, and therefore have continued to die. They were used as a sacrifice, a reminder of people's sin and salvation, until the New Testament, or new promise, was established by Jesus. It is only at death that the saved human returns to the presence of God; and quite possibly, so does the animal.

ANIMALS AS FOOD

Knowledge about the dietary needs of animals is ever

changing. Often people claim that domesticated or caged animals should eat what they would normally eat in the wild. Some people believe that certain animals are exclusively meat eaters. Others feel that they can and should be vegetarians. What is the answer? Does the Bible give us a clue about human and animal diets? It most certainly does.

Originally, it was God's plan for everything that could breathe to eat a vegetable diet.

> And to every beast of the earth, and to every bird of the sky and to every thing that moves on the earth which has life, *I have given* every green plant for food. (Gen. 1:30)

This includes the animals we now consider meat eaters or carnivores.

When Noah lived with all the animals on the ark, they ate vegetation.

> Also take with you every kind of food that is eaten, and store it up; and it shall serve as food for you and for them. (Gen. 6:21 NRSV)

This passage must refer to plants, since one does not "store up" animals. In the Age of the Lord, when Christ will come again and establish his kingdom on earth, animals will eat vegetation also; and all will be at peace on earth.

> And the cow and bear shall feed side by side, their young shall lie down together, and the lion shall eat straw like the ox. (Is. 11:70 AMP)

The Bible makes it clear that until God gave Noah permission to eat animals as well as plant life (*See* Gen. 9:3), it was God's plan that both people and animals be vegetarians. Vegetarianism can take place only at a time when death is removed from earth. There are two times mentioned in the Bible when there is no death. One was before the Fall of Adam and Eve in the Garden of Eden, and the other is after God sets up his thousand-year reign on earth.

The Bible also implies that it may be healthier for humans not to eat meat. We find this in the book of Daniel. Daniel was one of the young Jewish men selected to serve in the household of the Babylonian conqueror, King Nebuchadnezzar. As part of his preparation for service, he was ordered to eat the best food and drink the best wine that the king could provide. But Daniel, along with three other Jewish youths, chose not to do this because he did not want to disobey God by eating what was "unclean" according to Mosaic law. Instead he asked for water and vegetables. Their overseer was concerned that Daniel and his friends would not keep pace with the other youths who were under his care. So Daniel asked for ten days in which to prove to the overseer that his diet was better.

> 'Please test your servants for ten days, and let us be given some vegetables to eat and water to drink. Then let our appearance be observed in your presence and the appearance of the youths who are eating the king's choice food; and deal with your servants according to what you see.' So he listened to them in this matter and tested them for ten days. At the end of ten days their appearance seemed better and they were fatter than all the youths who had been eating the king's choice food. So the overseer continued to withhold their choice food and the wine they were to drink, and kept giving them vegetables. (Dan. 1:12-16)

Some people wonder if abstaining from meat is healthy; these passages show us that God can allow animals and humans to survive very well on vegetables.

The Bible makes it clear that eating meat is not a sin, but being a vegetarian is also okay. We know this because Genesis records that God gave Noah permission to eat meat:

'Everything that creeps on the ground and all the fish of the sea . . . Every moving thing that is alive shall be food for you; I give all to you as I gave the green plant.' (Gen. 9: 2-3)

Ryrie suggests a reason why God allowed man and animals to eat meat at this time:

The earth, radically affected by the Flood, confronted Noah with a more hostile environment. Longevity was decreased, habitable land areas reduced, oceans made more extensive, the crust of the earth made unstable and subject to seismic activity and the land laid barren. (pg. 16)

Noah and his family, as well as all the creatures of the earth, had to eat meat in order to survive since there was not enough vegetation available for them to eat plant matter alone. With all the radical changes to the earth's surface, it could be that many plants that existed before, could no longer survive after the Flood. This may also be one reason why some species of animals became extinct. Life was harsh for the survivors of the Flood, and food was less available.

Under these circumstances, God was showing kindness and providing for humans and animals by allowing them to eat meat. Therefore it is not a sin for humans and animals to eat meat.

We see that in the beginning, both humans and animals were vegetarians and were healthy. Remember that the conditions on earth during the long-ago time when animals and humans were vegetarians were not as harsh as after the Flood, creating the need to eat meat. At the end of this age, during the millennial reign of Christ, both animals and humans will be vegetarians again. In between those times, God has given both humans and animals the right to eat meat.

However, eating meat can only occur when there is physical death. When God removes physical death from the world, it will be for all his creatures; there will be no more killing animals for food.

5
THE OWNERSHIP & USE OF ANIMALS

A GROWING NUMBER of people and organizations would like to take pets away from people. They want to free animals from bondage to man; they desire that all working animals or pets should be set free to live in the wild. This would eliminate therapy animals, guide dogs, hearing dogs, and assistance dogs, as well as farm animals and pets.

This idea that people should not own animals is contrary to what the Bible teaches. God intended that animals and humans should live and work together. As discussed in chapter 1, God created certain animals to be wild and others to be domestic, even before he created humans!

The Bible states that God gave humankind dominion over all creation. This responsibility is a serious matter. According to *Webster's New World Dictionary*, "dominion" means "rule or the power to rule." God gave Adam the power and the right to rule over the earth, including all the animals.

When a person is in charge of or has authority over something, he must answer for the way he handles his responsibilities. The Bible states clearly many times that we will be accountable to God for the things that God has put in our care. One example of this is found in Matthew 25:14-20. In this parable, or story with a moral, a rich man gives some of his money to three servants to take care of for him while he is away. Two of the servants put the money to work, and double the amount that they were given. The third servant buries his portion and does nothing with it. When the master returns, he rewards the two who used the money wisely and punishes the one who did not.

According to the Bible, from the time of Adam until today humans have stewardship of the earth and everything in it. The Bible also makes it clear that we will be accountable to God for the way we treat the animals and the earth. When we look to Jesus as an example of lordship over the world, we see acts of service, love and kindness. Dominion does not give us the right to abuse or misuse what is in our care.

Dominion does give us the right to kill animals as necessary. We are given many examples of this in the Bible. As soon as Adam and Eve sinned and were expelled from the Garden of Eden, humans were allowed and, later, even required, to sacrifice animals. Actually, the first animal sacrifice occurred when God himself killed an animal to make clothes for Adam and Eve. (*See* chapter 4.) This event is the first recorded use of animals by humans. Later, when God instructed Noah to take two of every kind of animal into the ark to preserve them, he also instructed Noah to take seven pairs of each kind of clean animal for sacrificing.

The Bible fully endorses the use of animals for human purposes. There are many biblical examples of people using animals.

For instance, the prophet Elijah was sent by the Lord to anoint Elisha as a prophet to take his place. When Elijah first saw him, Elisha was using twelve pairs of oxen to plow his field (1 Kings 19:19).

Isaiah 5:28 refers to horses pulling chariots; Jeremiah 46:4 mentions the use of horses for riding. These are just a few of the many uses of animals mentioned in the Bible. People used animals for clothing, labor, transportation, and companionship.

Therefore we see that it is part of God's plan for humans and animals to live and work together, and that humans should use animals as needed, including for food.

As I work with search and rescue dogs, or as I watch dogs compete in sports events with their owners, it is obvious to me that the dogs love working with their owners. They are disappointed if they are left behind. This is not unique to dogs. I have known horses that were very upset if their owner rode another horse. Birds, too, enjoy performing the tricks that they have been taught. Some birds and other animals seem to enjoy playing tricks on their humans at unexpected times. Cats often prefer to sleep on their owners' laps instead of curling up alone. I have owned cats who loved to go for walks with me. The genuine enjoyment of these animals make it clear that it is not a hardship for them to work with their owners.

As we have seen, according to the Bible, we have charge over all the earth. We can use creation as we need to, but we must be good stewards of it. If it is necessary to kill animals we should do it in a humane way. It is our job to enhance, benefit and increase what God has created. But nowhere in the Bible is any part of creation put above humans.

Our bond and partnership with animals is ordained by God. Therefore no one should ever feel guilty for using an animal to help perform human tasks.

6
DO ANIMALS HAVE THE SAME RIGHTS & RULES AS HUMANS?

HUMANS HAVE DEVISED many laws in order to maintain a peaceable society. In light of this vast amount of human legislation, the topic of animal rights becomes a complicated one.

People have radically different views about what rights animals have, if any. Human rights are not the same worldwide; therefore it is no wonder that animal rights can easily become debatable as well. But again, the Bible does help us with this difficult topic.

God has created a complex set of rules that govern the universe. The rules of nature cannot be changed and they affect all things on earth. These are basic laws that fall into the realm of physics and nature, such as life, death, the needs of living things for food and water, the laws of gravity, and so forth. However, unlike the rules of nature, many of the detailed social rules that humans live by do not apply to animals; and some of the rules that animals follow do not apply to humans. For example, animals do not follow the same social rituals that humans follow. Various animals greet each other differently. Each species has its own way of greeting members of the same species. Each species also has its own unique mating ritual. Even among humans different groups of people have different rituals.

Yet God has given all humans some rules of conduct to follow. Many of these are the Ten Commandments and the laws given to the Levites. When humans do not follow these laws, it displeases God very much. Consider that only a few generations passed from Adam and Eve to Noah, when the world became so sinful that God was brokenhearted. He was so sad that he destroyed all that he had created with the Flood.

> The Lord saw that the wickedness of humankind was great in the earth, and that every inclination of the thoughts of their hearts was only evil continually. And the LORD was sorry that he had made humankind on the earth, and it grieved him to his heart. So the LORD said, 'I will blot out from the earth the human beings I have created—people together with animals and creeping things and birds of the air, for I am sorry that I have made them.' . . . 'For my part, I am going to bring a flood of waters on the earth, to destroy from under heaven all flesh in which is the breath of life; everything that is on the earth shall die.' (Gen. 6:5-7, 17 NRSV)

In the case of the Flood, all earth suffered because humans strayed from the rules or laws that God established. This event in the Bible does not indicate that anyone but humans had violated the rules, but God made some rules that do apply to both humans and animals. Our first example of such a rule occurs after the Flood. When God had made a new covenant with Noah, all of the earth and everything in it.

> 'Now behold, I Myself do establish My covenant with you, and with your descendants after you; and with every living creature that is with you, the birds, the cattle, and every beast of the earth with you; of all that comes out of the ark, even every beast of the earth.' (Gen. 9:9-10)

This covenant promised that God never again would destroy all earth's living things by water. As the sign of this promise God put the rainbow in the sky. While God was explaining the covenant to Noah, he said six times that the covenant includes all creatures of earth (*See* also chapter 3, "God Cares for Animals").

God's covenant with Noah and the animals established the stability of nature, and also showed that God considered the lives of humans and animals to be sacred. The covenant also showed that humans need rules to live by, and reminded them that wickedness cannot go unpunished. Before the Flood, wickedness filled the world; that is why everyone was destroyed except Noah and his family and the animals. Then right after the Flood God gave Noah rules to live by. These rules included one about homicide:

> For your own lifeblood I will surely require a reckoning: from every animal I will require it and from human beings, each one for the blood of another, I will require a reckoning for human life. (Gen. 9:5 NRSV)

The fact that this covenant was made for humans and animals, and that God will require a reckoning of every animal, makes it very plain that God expects both humans and animals to live by the rules he has established.

Another interesting passage in the Bible pertains to animals being punished for their behavior:

> If an ox gores a man or a woman to death, the ox shall surely be stoned and its flesh shall not be eaten; but the owner of the ox shall go unpunished. (Ex. 21:28)

This passage is for the protection of humans and other

animals as well as punishment for the offending animal. However, it is interesting that the owner of the animal may not eat the meat. This was punishment for the owner of the animal, since he had to give up what may have been valuable meat to either eat, sell or trade.

Even more interesting in light of the dog bite cases that we see today is what the Bible says regarding the ox owner who knows an ox has a tendency to attack humans.

> If, however, an ox was previously in the habit of goring and its owner has been warned, yet he does not confine it and it kills a man or a woman, the ox shall be stoned and its owner also shall be put to death. If a ransom is demanded of him, then he shall give for the redemption of his life whatever is demanded of him. Whether it gores a son or a daughter, it shall be done to him according to the same rule. (Ex. 21:29-31)

According to the Bible, the owner of the animal is held responsible for the action of the animal.

Humans have the right to own and use animals, but animals do not have similar rights to control humans. If an animal tries to coerce a human, it is dealt with by training, or by placing the animal in a situation where it can be controlled. It is the job of animal trainers and behaviorists to teach animals how to get along with and obey the wishes of their human owners.

As an animal behavior consultant, I have had clients come to me with requests to alter their pets' behavior in many different ways. One client may want me to teach a dog not to bark often; yet another client may not mind a barking dog, but rather wants his dog to stay off the furniture. The rules which dogs must follow to live in their owners' homes can vary widely.

Whatever the specific rule, God has directed that the manner in which humans treat animals must be humane and kind. The animals that were created as domestic are expected by God to obey and live in harmony with humans.

The wild animals are not expected to live in harmony with humans, yet they too have rules to follow.

For example, each species of bird will have a mating ritual unique to its species. They will build nests according to their needs. Animals such as horses, cows, deer, and other more social species live in groups. Other animals such as wolves, will alternately live in packs or alone, depending on the time of year and the need. One example that most people have seen is the flocking of birds when they migrate. They have a specific order for this procedure. For example, when geese fly in a vee formation, they take turns flying in the lead or at the head of the vee which is the most difficult position, so they can fly in the less difficult positions for a while and rest. If geese did not follow the rules of migration, many would die.

Although the Bible does not tell us that animals will give an account of themselves to God, they must follow the rules of living that God has set forth. If there were no rules, there would be no order to the world, and life would be impossible.

Finally, consider that both humans and animals were made from the same material, were given many of the same blessings, and physically function in much the same way. This would imply that God did not make humans to be entirely different from animals. Therefore it is logical to assume that animals and humans would follow similar rules.

7
CAN ANIMALS THINK?

FIRST LET ME ask, exactly what is "thinking"? This is a question that has been pondered, studied and analyzed for hundreds of years. In the late 1500s, René Descartes, a famous philosopher, scientist, mathematician and writer, considered to be the father of modern philosophy, wrestled with this problem. He came to the famous conclusion, "I think, therefore I am." More recently psychologists and scientists have defined thinking as the act of being aware of oneself, and one's environment. It is the ability to learn, analyze data, and express feelings. Today scientists use the term "episodic memory" to describe the ability to recall the past, to be aware of the present, and to plan for the future.

The real challenge in analyzing any species of animal, bird, or insect's ability to think is to develop tests that meet the scientific model (repeatable and stable) that give us the ability to test other species. Scientists must do this without the benefit of a common language, which has made studies very difficult. Thus it is still one of the mysteries of an animal lover's life: do animals think? And if so, what do they think about?

For a long time scientists believed that animals did not think at all. In the book, *Companion Dog Training*, dog trainer Hans Tossuttii stated,

> For years controversy has raged regarding the dog's ability to reason. And because of the close bond of affection

between every dog owner and their dog, many have held to what they believe to be true, that the dog can and does reason. But I agree with those scientists and intelligent students who claim that he cannot.

However, since the time of that book's publishing in 1948, scientists have discovered that animals do think and communicate after all.

A recent study claims that dogs are smarter than had previously been thought. Scientists at the University of California, Davis have found that dogs communicate using different pitches in their barks.

Another test at Brazil's Pontifical Catholic University indicates that dogs have basic counting ability.

In yet another study, German researchers tested one dog and found that it understood over 200 words. This study also demonstrated that the dog could figure out what new words meant.

Researchers have taught primates how to use sign language to communicate. The result of these efforts has convinced most of the scientific community that animals can think, reason and, if given the means, communicate. Scientists are even now starting to believe that not only can animals think, but they also have feelings, emotions, and the ability to demonstrate their feelings.

Natural History Magazine published an article whose title sums up the current belief about this. The article is called "Tete-a -Tete, Can One Animal Tell Another How It Feels? Eloquently."

That even sea life is smarter than we thought is evidenced in another study summarized in the same magazine.[1] The study concluded that the crabs showed good spatial knowledge and cognitive memory. In other words, even crabs can think, make decisions and recall information.

Alison Jolly wrote an article, "A New Science That Sees Animals as Conscious Beings," in which she states that cognitive ethologist Donald Griffin believes that primates can lie, and that even bees can think. These are not lone voices in the wilderness. Researcher Joan Stephenson Graf found that animals can recognize their family members. They not only recognize their parents and siblings, but can distinguish cousins from aunts, and family from strangers. Author Kenneth Jon Rose believes that some animals may be just as bright as some people.

Recently, Eugene Linden, in his book, *The Parrot's Lament*, tells of an interesting experiment. An ecologist named James Gould took some bees and flowers into the middle of a lake in a rowboat, and at the same time placed another group of bees close to shore at a feeder. When the bees from the rowboat flew to the bees near the shore, they gave the signal that communicates the direction of the flowers, which were in the middle of the lake. What is interesting is that the bees near the shore did not believe the bees from the rowboat. Few bees showed up at the rowboat in the middle of the lake, yet many bees went to the feeder in a boat near the shore.

What does this mean? It shows that even bees have some level of awareness and are not totally and only hardwired with instinct. The bees on the shore decided not to believe the message given by the bees from the middle of the lake. This shows an awareness of the water, and of the fact that pollen-bearing flowers do not grow in water. They made the decision that the bees from the middle of the lake were wrong.

A very interesting commentary in the *Los Angeles Times* states:

What . . . researchers are finding is that many of our fellow creatures are more like us than we had ever imagined. They feel pain, suffer and experience stress, affection, excitement and even love, and these findings are changing how we view animals.

More recently, an article in the October 27, 2006 issue of *Wall Street Journal* titled "What Your Pet Is Thinking," goes even further. The article tells how tests have demonstrated that animals are capable of thinking about their thoughts, or have consciousness. The article also states that ethologists (scientists who study animal behavior) have shown that animals can count, understand cause and effect, form abstractions, solve problems, use tools, and in some cases deceive.

These findings show us that we cannot make assumptions about God's creation. All of the research sheds new light on what the Bible says about animals. How do the accounts of animals in the Bible compare to the latest scientific research?

We have a wonderful example of a donkey's cognitive abilities in the book of Numbers.

Balaam was well known for his abilities as a prophet. Therefore he was summoned by King Balak of Moab, an enemy of the Israelites. The king wanted to pay Balaam to curse the Israelites. Although Balaam knew who the true God was, he had made a business of practicing omens and soothsaying, which was against God's express commands. When Balaam received the request to curse the Israelites, he invited the messengers to spend the night with him while he prayed to the God of Israel.

During the night God told Balaam that he was *not* to curse the Israelites. Balaam told the messengers that he would not go with them, and they in turn told the king. When the king heard this, he increased the fee for Balaam. This tempted Balaam and he again asked God if he could go to the king. This time God told him that he could go, but that he could only say the words that God put in his mouth.

Balaam hoped that God would change his mind about cursing the Israelites, because he wanted the fee promised to him by the king of Moab. What was in Balaam's heart angered God, so on the way to the city, an angel of the Lord stood in the road. Balaam could not see the angel, but his donkey could and it refused to continue. Three times the angel blocked the way and three times the donkey tried to turn away. The donkey went into a field, then crushed Balaam's foot against a wall and finally lay down and refused to move.

Each time the donkey refused to obey him, Balaam hit the donkey. What happened next is very curious.

Then the LORD opened the mouth of the donkey, and it said to Balaam, 'What have I done to you, that you have struck me these three times?' Balaam said to the donkey, 'Because you have made a fool of me! I wish I had a sword in my hand! I would kill you right now!' But the donkey said to Balaam, 'Am I not your donkey, which you have ridden all your life to this day? Have I been in the habit of treating you this way?' And he said, 'No.'
Then the LORD opened the eyes of Balaam and he saw the angel of the LORD standing in the road, with his drawn sword in his hand; and he bowed down, falling on his face. The angel of the LORD said to him, 'Why have you struck your donkey these three times? I have come out as an adversary, because your way is perverse before me. The donkey saw me, and turned away from me these three times. If it had not turned away from me, surely just now I would have killed you and let it live.' (Num. 22:28-33 NRSV)

In this exciting passage Balaam was not surprised that the donkey talked. During Balaam's time, Satan and his demons may have used animals as well as statues to communicate to people, at times making these things appear to talk. This would explain why Balaam was not surprised when his donkey talked to him. However, since the Bible tells us that God opened the donkey's mouth, we know this particular incident was not a demonic act.

What the Bible says and implies about the donkey is interesting. The donkey's questions show that the donkey could think, knew what was right from wrong, and recognized the angel for what it was.

The donkey asked Balaam why he hit it. The donkey's logic about its lifelong service to Balaam meriting kind treatment from him shows a keen awareness of the past, as well as a sense of justice. All of this demonstrates that the donkey could think.[2]

The donkey could see the angel and knew what would happen if it continued on the road. The donkey understood the purpose of the angel and that the angel came from God. The donkey was not afraid of the angel, but was protecting Balaam from the angel who was acting according to God's direction.

The donkey is given credit for its thought and understanding. The Bible does not say that God gave the donkey special wisdom and understanding, but only that God "opened the mouth of the donkey" to allow it to communicate to Balaam.

The Bible also did not say that God "opened the donkey's eyes" to see the angel, as he did with Balaam.

Does that imply that animals can see the spirit world? If Balaam's donkey had never seen angels or did not know what it saw, wouldn't the donkey have been afraid? How did the donkey know what the angel was there to do?

When Jesus was born the angels appeared to the shepherds in the fields (Luke 2:8-16). The shepherds were afraid but apparently the sheep were not; they did not run away. Perhaps they recognized the messengers of God.

In the book of Job, the Bible gives us another look at the mind of animals.

> But now ask the beasts, and let them teach you; and the birds of the heavens, and let them tell you. Or speak to the earth, and let it teach you; and let the fish of the sea declare to you. Who among all these does not know that the hand of the Lord has done this, in whose hand is the life of every living thing and the breath of all mankind? (Job 12:7-10)

In this situation Job has been mocked by his friend Zophar about his misfortune. Job tells Zophar that even the animals are smarter than he is because the animals, and even the earth, know that misfortune comes from the hand of God. Job clearly understood that God made his covenant with all of creation, and that all of creation is aware of God. Some might feel that Job is being a bit of a smart aleck toward his friend; but later on God uses the same example when he reprimands Job.

Modern science and research agree with the Bible to give us a strong possibility that animals can communicate with God or at least are aware of the existence of God, that they are aware of their life circumstances, and that they can think.

This has been evident many times in my own experience training and working with search and rescue (SAR) dogs. In training, we can never set up the exact circumstances that we will encounter on an actual mission. Yet time after time, the dogs have assessed the situation, and then adapted to it to solve the problem. Dogs exhibit different behavior once they get a few real missions "under their belt." They never work in training quite the same again. Some dogs who have been on real missions have a different, more serious attitude during the real mission, and a more relaxed, playful one during training sessions. One of my own dogs would play around during training, but never during a real mission.

One time my husband and I were giving a demonstration in a very small area. The only way we could demonstrate the mechanics of how an air-scenting dog works was to set up a series of cardboard boxes and hide someone in one of them. My husband took his SAR dog Ness into the ring.

When my husband told Ness to find the hidden person, Ness gave my husband a look that clearly said, "What? You've got to be kidding!" The people in the crowd who saw his look all laughed at the same time. They knew what the look meant.

Then to show his frustration at such a ridiculous problem, Ness did something that he has never done before or since. He ran right to the box with the person hidden inside and ripped the box to shreds.

Almost everyone who lives with or around animals will agree that animals can think and experience emotions, and will try to communicate with other living beings. Human science is finally catching on to what the Bible told us over two thousand years ago.

It is evident to us that animals not only think, but find pleasure in their lives on earth. One only has to watch puppies or kittens playing to see that. The affection that our pets give us is another example. Think of a cat lying on a person's lap, purring with contentment. Or a horse who presses his forehead against the chest of his human partner. Today we have captured the behavior of many types of animals on film. We have the unique opportunity to see the joy and grief that animals experience. For example, the loyalty and love that elephants exhibit show the depth of their feelings. God has given animals the ability to think and to feel emotions.

8
UNDERSTANDING & COMMUNICATING WITH ANIMALS

ALL ANIMAL LOVERS may wish at times that they could talk with their animals so they could better understand the animals. Many books have been written in an attempt to explain how to do this. Some are genuine, well-researched theories, while others are just gimmicks to sell books; however, the bottom line is that they sell because animal lovers have a keen interest in understanding and bonding closer to the animals they care about.

The book of Job gives us a wonderful glimpse into the minds of animals. The Bible tells us that Job was a wealthy man who was also considered to be a good man. God found Job blameless, upright, and God-fearing, a man who turned away from evil. Because of this, Satan challenged God about Job's upstanding life by claiming that Job was only good because he had everything in life a person could want. Satan thought that if Job had troubles he would turn away from God.

In answer to this challenge, God gave Satan permission to test Job's righteousness. Satan caused Job to lose all that he owned, including his children. Next, Satan afflicted Job with painful physical ailments.

Remember, Job had no idea why these horrible things were happening to him. He didn't know of the bargain Satan had struck with God; he didn't know God had boasted about him; he didn't know that he would someday receive back everything he

had lost and more. When Job cried out to God, God answered
by challenging Job's understanding of his situation. Because Job
thought he knew about the world he lived in, God used all
of creation as an object lesson to show Job that he did not
understand much at all, least of all what had happened to him.

In revealing the nature of animals to Job, God has given us
insight about the mind, behavior and heart of the animals he
created. These descriptions are the direct words of God to Job:

Who has let the wild ass go free? Who has loosed the
bonds of the swift ass, to whom I have given the steppe
for its home, the salt land for its dwelling place? It scorns
the tumult of the city; it does not hear the shouts of
the driver. It ranges the mountains as its pasture, and it
searches after every green thing. Is the wild ox willing
to serve you? Will it spend the night at your crib? Can
you tie it in the furrow with ropes, or will it harrow
the valleys after you? Will you depend on it because its
strength is great, and will you hand over your labor to it?
Do you have faith in it that it will return, and bring your
grain to your threshing floor?

The ostrich's wings flap wildly; though its pinions lack
plumage. For it leaves its eggs to the earth, and lets them
be warmed on the ground, forgetting that a foot may
crush them, and that a wild animal may crush them. It
deals cruelly with its young, as if they were not its own;
though its labor should be in vain, yet it has no fear;
because God has made it forget wisdom, and given it no
share in understanding. When it spreads its plumes aloft,
it laughs at the horse and its rider.

Do you give the horse its might? Do you clothe its
neck with mane? Do you make it leap like the locust?

Its majestic snorting is terrible. It paws violently, exults mightily; it goes out to meet the weapons. It laughs at fear, and is not dismayed; it does not turn back from the sword. Upon it rattle the quiver, the flashing spear, and the javelin. With fierceness and rage it swallows the ground; it cannot stand still at the sound of the trumpet. When the trumpet sounds, it says, 'Aha!' From a distance it smells the battle, the thunder of the captains, and the shouting.

Is it by your wisdom that the hawk soars, and spreads its wings toward the south? Is it at your command that the eagle mounts up and makes its nest on high? It lives on the rock and makes its home in the fastness of the rocky crag. (Job 39: 5-28 NRSV)

God begins by explaining to Job that humans cannot domesticate some animals. God points this out when he talks about the wild ass and the wild ox. Then God demonstrates that he takes care of all of the animals he created. He enjoys them and delights in them.

God's rhetorical questions emphasize that humans cannot fully understand animals, what they do and why they do it. He has not intended for humans to have complete understanding of the animal world. Yet people have always had a longing to communicate with and understand animals. Perhaps this is because that was God's original plan. There was total harmony and peace in the Garden of Eden; there Adam and Eve could communicate with and understand the animals. After the first man and woman fell from grace, and God expelled them from the Garden, they lost the ability to understand and communicate with animals.

Many of today's scientific tools and processes allow us to study animals, to interact with them and observe their behavior.

For example, some primates have been taught to communicate in sign language, giving us new information about their nature and minds.

These studies have given us a depth of understanding that was only imagined in past decades. Yet these methods are primitive at best; they are mere teasers. Will God allow us ever to fully understand animals? Based on what the Bible says, it is not likely. However, the information we have learned about the mind of animals does clarify some of the statements and events in the Bible.

No matter how advanced we become, or how much we study, I believe we will never know for sure what is in the mind of an animal, including our pets.

Many people who love animals also have a deep desire to express their feelings to their pet. This is one of the reasons why the Dr. Doolittle theme has endured for so long. It is also evidenced by the popularity of animal communicators, people who claim to communicate with animals through psychic means. Why would God deny us such a wonderful experience?

But did he?

As discussed earlier, it is possible that in the Garden of Eden, before the Fall, Adam and Eve could communicate with animals. Eve was not surprised when the serpent spoke to her. The biblical account suggests that this was not an uncommon event; communicating with animals may have been a normal part of life in Eden.

Later, Noah also worked with the creatures that entered the ark. It would appear as though there was some form of communication or understanding in this situation. Although the Bible doesn't specifically mention verbal communication between Noah and the animals, it never says that Noah had to train all of the animals to respond to him, either.

But let me ask: If we could talk freely to animals, how would we live in peace and do what we have to do with animals? Keep in mind that communication would be a two-way street, so the animals would understand what we say as well. Then imagine the confusion and unpleasantness that would exist if we could understand the meaning of animal sounds and they could understand all of our words.

For example, we know that many sounds birds make are not happy, sweet singing, as we hear them, but challenges to other birds to stay out of their territory. What if the beautiful song a caged canary sings is actually one of woe and sadness, or a lonely call for a companion? This would not make owning the canary very pleasant and the singing that we enjoy could become troublesome.

Another biblical incident illustrates God's plan for human communication, the account of the Tower of Babel in Genesis chapter 11. People banded together and decided to build a tower that reached to the heavens. Their purpose was not to worship God but to become like the "gods" themselves.

The Bible tells us that at that time everyone spoke the same language. Because of their evil desires, God caused the people to speak different languages. God took away the ability for people to communicate freely with each other. Why then would he want us to be able to talk to animals?

The tower and city of Babel (later to become Babylon) was built to unite the people of earth; this was against the direct order of God to spread and populate the world.

> The Lord came down to see the city and the tower which the sons of men had built. The Lord said, 'Behold, they are one people, and they all have the same language. And this is what they began to do, and now nothing which

they purpose to do will be impossible for them. Come,
let Us go down and there confuse their language, that
they may not understand one another's speech.' So the
Lord scattered them abroad from there over the face
of the whole earth; and they stopped building the city.
Therefore its name was called Babel, because there the
Lord confused the language of the whole earth; and from
there the Lord scattered them abroad over the face of the
whole earth. (Gen. 11:5-9)

If God did not want all peoples to be able to communicate
with spoken words, he obviously did not want people and animals
to communicate either. The example of the Tower of Babel is
not intended to imply that animals are evil or that their communication with humans would result in animals and humans
plotting evil deeds, but merely to illustrate that God clearly made
it difficult for humans to communicate. Since God does not
want humans to have total freedom of communication, and since
humans cannot talk to animals, it is reasonable to conclude that
he does not give humans the ability to talk to animals.

Another possible reason God prevents us from communicating with animals may be their understanding of God. As we have
discussed, the first physical death on earth was that of an animal,
and the world was cursed because of the sin of Adam and Eve.
If animals are aware of God and at least some of the order of
creation, then they might not have very nice things to say to
us. Even though animals are not equal to humans by God's
directive, it is possible that they might not approve of some of the
things we do. Animal lovers know by their behavior that animals
do have likes and dislikes. How far could those likes, dislikes
and opinions go if there were complete understanding between
humans and animals? Also if animals understood all of people's

plans for them, such as raising them for food, what do you think the results would be?

Consider that if animals understood our spoken words, they might not be willing to obey the wishes of their owners. As many pet owners know, this happens anyway, which is why we have to teach animals to obey. But imagine if your pets could understand your conversation when you tell someone that in an hour the pet is going to the veterinarian for yearly shots. I can imagine the creative pet finding a hiding place that would cause the pet owner to miss the appointment.

What about the people who claim to be able to communicate with animals through psychic means? It is not for us to judge what is in the hearts of other people. Only God can do that. But we can use what the Bible says as a guide. There are only two instances recorded in the Bible where an animal talked to a human. The first was when the serpent talked to Eve in the Garden of Eden (*See* chapter 11). The other is Balaam's donkey. We are told that God opened the donkey's mouth and let the animal talk; therefore we know that it was not by demon power, but by the will of God. See chapter 7, "Can Animals Think?", for a detailed description of this incident.

In Numbers chapter 22 we see that Balaam also used psychic means to cast spells and possibly talk with animals. But was he really talking with animals, or to demons who talked *through* animals? The Bible tells us that what psychics do is not from God. In fact, the Bible tells us that this practice is the work of demons:

> There shall not be found among you anyone who makes his son or daughter pass through fire, one who uses divination, one who practices witchcraft, or one who interprets omens, or a sorcerer, or one who casts a spell,

or a medium, or a spiritist, or one who calls up the dead. For whoever does these things is detestable to the Lord. (Deut. 18:10-12)

Based on how the Bible describes the activities of psychics, it is evident that well-meaning but misled people who claim to be able to use psychic means to communicate with animals are not really communicating with animals, but demons. Often these people do not realize what they are dealing with. The Bible warns us against using these people. God did not give us the ability to communicate with animals. Psychics are not able to do so, either, whether the animal is alive or dead.[1]

In general, it is apparent that God does not want humans to be able to directly and fully communicate with animals. However, God has given some people the gift of understanding animal behavior well enough to help them adapt to living with humans. These people are usually animal trainers or behaviorists. They use their knowledge of the animal and proven techniques, not psychic means, to understand and solve training and behavior problems.

But take heart, all you who long to talk to animals; there is strong evidence in the Bible that in the Garden of Eden before the Fall, humans and animals got along peacefully and communicated with each other; and in the future thousand-year reign of God, the same conditions will apply as in the Garden of Eden.

For now, even though your dog may hide in the closet when you say "bath" and jump up and down with glee when you say "walk," your pet cannot fully understand you and you cannot totally communicate with your pet. And, as in all things God has planned, it is for our good.

Great horned owl mom and baby
Photo © Karen Webster, PEAC

Sheep are often mentioned in the Bible.

A parrot named Samantha
Photo © Karen Webster, PEAC

A raven fed the prophet Elijah.
Photo © Karen Webster, PEAC

Harbor seal   *Photo © Karen Webster, PEAC*

Butterfly, an example of God's creativity

GOD CREATED THE BIRDS OF THE AIR, THE CREATURES OF THE SEA, LAND ANIMALS AND CREEPING THINGS, AND GOD "SAW THAT IT WAS GOOD" (GEN. 1:25).

One way animals minister to humans today is by providing a bridge for children and adults who suffer from physical and mental ailments.

Hero, a certified Therapy Rottweiler, provides support to mentally-challenged school children, in the library *(left)* and listening to a child read *(below)*.

Photos by Heddie S. Leger, courtesy of The PawZone

The author as a young girl with her cat, Puff.

"Scout" at night. It is possible that animals have an awareness of God.

Photo by Jean Edwards

Horses work with humans in many ways and seem to enjoy the companionship.

Photos courtesy of Bev Coons

DOMESTIC ANIMALS ARE GOOD COMPANIONS AND HELPERS

Grizzly bear

Given a choice, lions do not like to attack humans. *Photo by Alisann Crough*

God told Job about many animals, including ostriches. *Photo by Alisann Crough*

Adam witnessed the love and loyalty animal families often have for each other, such as this elephant mom and baby. *Photo by Alisann Crough*

A tiger's piercing eyes—a fearsome sight. Yet none of God's creatures are evil. *Photo by Andrija Jezdic*

GOD CARES FOR, AND TEACHES US THROUGH, THE WILD ANIMALS

Red squirrel and Bohemian waxwing   *Photos © Karen Webster, PEAC*

Red-eyed
tree frog

*Photo ©
Karen
Webster,
PEAC*

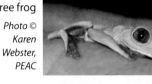

Cat friends
napping.

*Photo ©
Janet
Velenovsky
CPDT CDBC-TAC*

Donkeys named Eeyore and Shadow.
The Bible often refers to donkeys, and one
talked to Balaam.   *Photo by Alisann Crough*

All animals, including these zebras, obey the rules God established.   *Photo by Alisann Crough*

GOD CREATED A WONDERFUL VARIETY OF CREATURES
FOR HIS PLEASURE AND OURS

9
GOD COMMUNICATES WITH ANIMALS

WE HAVE ALL heard or read stories about an animal showing up
at just the right time to save or help a human. We have also
heard stories of an untrained animal helping someone in need,
even when the person is a stranger to the animal. How could this
be? How can an animal with no training know what to do? Some
people believe the animals have psychic power, but the Bible
refutes this. Still others believe that an animal is able to assess the
situation on its own and come up with a solution.

I think the latter is the case: the animal understands the
situation and acts. I also believe that in some cases, the animal
is guided by God.

For example, when we lived in the country my neighbor's
property bordered on a swift creek. The creek was too wide to
cross over and too swift to safely walk in. The creekbanks were
lined by many trees; and as often happens, over time the water
undermined the roots of a large tree and it fell toward the creek.
The tree was almost horizontal but the banks of the creek kept it
well above the water. My neighbor had four young grandchildren
who often came to visit. One day while I was working in my
garden, my dog quietly slipped away and ran to my neighbor's
yard. It turned out that the children had climbed out onto the
tree. My dog did not like this and tried to lure the children off
the tree. When this did not work, he went to my neighbor's house

and barked. He managed to persuade my neighbor to follow him, then led her straight to the children and the tree.

Here is another example. My neighbor (the same one) and I each had a flock of chickens and we both let our chickens range free. One day while I was cutting the grass I saw my dog trot over to my neighbor's house. The dog saw that my neighbor's chickens were foraging close to the road, so he very gently grouped her chickens into a tight flock and moved them all toward their own hen house. The amazing thing is, he had never been trained to herd chickens. Also, her chickens were not familiar with my dog, yet he was able to move them without frightening them.

Is it possible that God directs animals to do what they do? How might God communicate with animals, and under what circumstances? These are valid questions; the answers will help us understand the animals' relationship with God and how they are used by him.

Let me start by giving a working definition of the term "communication." For the purposes of this discussion, communication is nothing more than the act of sending messages back and forth. The message may be in the form of a signal, spoken sounds, written words, looks, or gestures. Communication may also be in the form of an understanding between two beings that in some cases can be a feeling.

Communication, then, can take many forms, some of which humans do not clearly understand.

I once witnessed an amazing animal communication event. I used to race Siberian Huskies. We would often race the teams through acres of woods with paths that made good sled dog trails. Because we had to share these trails, the team owners would stake out their teams until it was time to harness them to run. A stake-out was often a chain with large links, attached between two trees. Staking to large trees was the most practical method, since a whole team of Huskies were strong enough to move almost anything else. Each dog was then attached by a smaller chain and clip to the large chain, forming a line of dogs that could not quite touch each other (to prevent tangles).

As I walked toward my own dogs, I saw two teams staked out opposite each other. There was a small trail between them. The dogs were milling around, not paying attention to each other or the other team. Then quite suddenly, almost magically, all the dogs stopped what they were doing, and each dog on both teams sat in a row looking at each other across the narrow trail. I paid very close attention since this was unusual.

Then without any apparent signal, one team, all at exactly the same moment, started to sing the same song. Husky songs are a series of howls at various pitches. Each dog was singing the same pitch, starting at the exact same moment and ending at the same moment. When the first team finished, the second team replied, all starting at the same time, singing the same song, and ending at the same time. Then they all went back to milling around as before.

It was one of the most amazing things I have ever witnessed. Their singing was as perfectly in tune and in time with each other as a symphony orchestra. What confounded me the most was that I could not detect any signal between the dogs or between the teams. As an animal behaviorist, I realize that they must have signaled each other in some manner, but to this day, I have not been able to detect how.

This experience taught me the important lesson that, no matter how hard we try, we do not understand all there is to know about God's creatures. It also taught me early in my career that there are forms of communication between animals that we may never understand. I am thankful for the experience.

Besides forms of communication among themselves, the

Bible clearly shows us that God himself communicates with animals. The way God uses animals and how they react to him give us insight into the mind and intelligence of animals. Communication with God demonstrates that animals have:

1) the ability to think.
2) an awareness of God's presence.
3) at least some knowledge of who God is.
4) the ability to understand God's commands.

To understand how God communicates with animals, we should not think of communication only in ways that are common to humans, such as the written/spoken word, gestures, pictures, and music.

Communication is a complex matter that can take many forms, some of which are a mystery to humans. To illustrate this concept let's look at some examples.

Consider birds, such as the robin. This is a species of bird that does not typically flock the way chickens, geese or ducks do. Yet at the time of migration, robins will form a flock and migrate together. How does each individual bird know when and where to meet? How do they all know which route to take and how far to fly? Consider schools of fish. How do they know to swim in the same direction, or even stay together? The mystery is not unique to birds, but applies to any species of animal or insect that migrates. Think of the Monarch butterfly.

Furthermore, communication is not limited to birds, animals and insects. Plants also have ways of interacting and sharing information.

When a disease or insect attacks some tree species, the first tree that is attacked will emit a chemical that other trees of the same species can detect. This chemical triggers a warning signal in the neighboring trees, allowing them to protect themselves from the attacking agents. The trees communicate with each other through a chemical signal.

Another means of communication is through light and color. The following is quoted from an article that describes plants' ability to detect and react to colors not visible to the human eye:

> Plants 'see' far-red, a color beyond human vision which is in the light spectrum, as a signal to increase shoot growth. Using plastic mulch that reflects far-red, researcher Michael Kasperbauer tricks tomato plants into sensing competitors nearby. The tomatoes grow bigger and ripen earlier. Other colored mulches affect flavor and nutrient content. (*National Geographic*, July 1999, pg. 82)

Just how do plants see the color? Similarly, an earthworm has no eyes, yet it can detect light. We may never know the answer to how tomatoes and earthworms see, yet we know they react to their environment, and that is a form of communication.

On the radio program Creation Moments, Ian Taylor reported that scientists conducted experiments to show that plants have feeling and memory. Using the same variety of young plants, they punched two pin holes in the same leaf of each plant. Then they stripped the leaves off the plants. Without exception, all the plants produced new leaves—except where the injured leaves had been.

This experiment is further enhanced by studies in the field of neurobiology, where scientists have determined that plants have "brains," can detect friends and foes, and react accordingly. Patrick Johnson states in "New Research Opens a Window of the Minds of Plants," printed in the *Christian Science Monitor* (March 3, 2005), that mustard weed cannot find its way in the world if its starchy "brain" (the root-tip-statolith) is cut off. These discoveries give new meaning to the following Scripture:

> For we know that the whole creation groans and suffers the pains of childbirth together until now. (Rom. 8:22)

Is it possible that all of creation knows the Creator? That in some way all of life and the very earth itself wait and groan for the creation of the new heaven and new earth promised by God, an existence similar to life in the Garden of Eden, with no pain and suffering?

As far back as the book of Genesis, the Bible speaks about God talking to animals.

> God blessed them saying, 'Be fruitful and multiply, and fill the waters in the seas, and let birds multiply on the earth.' (Gen. 1:22)

This is the first time in the Bible that we read of God talking directly to the animals. He would not speak to them if they could not understand and obey.

We are given another example of God's communication with animals in 1 Samuel 6:1-12. The Philistines, a people hostile to God's people, had captured the Ark of the Covenant, the holy symbol of God's presence with his people. The Philistines believed that because they had defeated the Israelite army, they had also defeated Yahweh, the Israelites' God. To them it showed the superiority of their own god, Baal. They placed the Ark of the Covenant inside the temple of their god. As a result, a plague broke out among the Philistines. They consulted their priests, who decided to test the strength of the God of the Israelites.

They separated cows, which were untrained as draft animals,

from their calves and yoked them to a cart which carried the Ark. They then let the yoked animals walk. If the mothers went back to their calves, they would know that the Ark was nothing and Yahweh was powerless. But if the cows took the Ark to the Israelites, they would know Yahweh was stronger than their gods.

> And the cows took the straight way in the direction of Beth Shemesh, they went along the highway, lowing as they went, and did not turn aside to the right or the left. And the lords of the Philistines followed them to the border of Beth-shemesh. (1 Sam. 6:12)

To train a new cow to the yoke, common practice was to yoke the untrained with a trained cow. That way the trained animal helped to control the efforts of the untrained one to pull right or left, in an attempt to get out of the yoke. When this passage says the cows neither turned to the right or left, it means that they pulled together and that they followed the correct road. The fact that the untrained cows pulled together and did not turn to the right or left, leaving the road, shows that God was in control. We can easily infer that God somehow showed the cows how to behave to take the ark back to the Israelites. Keep in mind that God had to direct the cows where to go since these cows, or oxen, did not belong to the Israelites and therefore would not know the correct road to take. Also note that the animals obeyed God's will despite the fact that their natural desire would be to go back to their young.

In another example from 1 Kings 17, God communicated to ravens, directing them to do something that is unnatural for them. God had told the prophet Elijah to live by a brook while he sent a severe drought upon the land of Israel. God commanded the ravens to feed Elijah. The Bible does not tell us where the ravens found food for Elijah; we do know that the drought was so severe that people and animals died. The ravens, too, must have suffered. Yet they brought food to Elijah. The ravens had to give up scarce food and overcome their fear of humans, showing us that they must have been acting on God's orders.

'It shall be that you shall drink of the brook, and I have commanded the ravens to provide for you there.' So he went and did according to the word of the Lord, for he went and lived by the brook Cherith, which is east of the Jordan. The ravens brought him bread and meat in the morning and bread and meat in the evening, and he would drink from the brook. (1 Kings 17:4-6)

Another reference to communication between God and ravens is found in the book of Job, when God reminds Job of his own sovereignty over all creation.

Who provides for the raven its prey, when its young ones cry to God . . . ? (Job 38:41 NRSV)

Here is dialogue between God and the raven. The infant ravens call to God for help and God responds. This shows us that the raven is aware of God, who he is and what he does. It also shows us that God is aware of his creatures.

It is not unusual for adult ravens to forget about their young and not feed them. God is telling Job that not only does he know when this happens, but he also provides the young birds with prey, or food, so that they do not die.

The psalmist tells us that not only does God control all of creation, but the spirit of every living thing depends upon God for its life and food:

The young lions roar after their prey and seek their food
from God. . . . They all wait for You to give them their
food in due season. You give to them, they gather it up;
You open Your hand, they are satisfied with good. You
hide Your face, they are dismayed; You take away their
spirit, they expire and return to their dust. You send forth
Your Spirit, they are created; And You renew the face of
the ground. (Ps. 104:21, 27-29)

In this passage, humans have been punished for their sins and
the animals also suffer:

Even the wild animals cry to you because the water-
courses are dried up, and fire has devoured the pastures of
the wilderness. (Joel 1:20 NRSV)

In their suffering, the animals cry to God for water and food.
They must recognize that he is their caregiver, and that he hears
them when they cry to him.

Another example that demonstrates both cognitive awareness
in animals and God's communication with them is when God
allowed Adam to name all the animals. God thus demonstrated
to the animals that Adam had the right to rule them. The
animals must have understood the concept and been aware of the
situation. This shows that God did not create animals with the
knowledge of subjection to humans—they had to be shown. It
also demonstrates that animals are not totally hard wired with
instinct. They do have many instincts; but they can also think.[1]

Another example of this is found in the Flood account:

On the very same day Noah with his sons, Shem and Ham
and Japheth, and Noah's wife and the three wives of his

> sons entered the ark, they and every wild animal of every
> kind, and all domestic animals of every kind, and every
> creeping thing that creeps on the earth, and every bird of
> every kind—every bird, every winged creature. They went
> into the ark with Noah, two and two of all flesh in which
> there was the breath of life. (Gen 7:13-15 NRSV)

God commanded seven of every clean animal and two of every
other kind of creature on the face of the earth to report to Noah.
All of the animals had to obey Noah as they entered the ark and
during the time that they lived in the ark. The animals heard and
obeyed God, which shows that he communicated to them.

The Amplified Bible notes: "Noah had many years in which
to interest travelers in securing these animals for him." Given
the vast number of species that exist in the world, and all of the
varieties of these species, it is questionable whether humans could
have collected them to bring to Noah. Yet the Bible does not
state that Noah obtained the animals himself or had other people
do it for him. Note that these verses say the animals will come to
Noah, not that he will search them out.

> Of the birds after their kind, and of the animals after
> their kind, of every creeping thing of the ground after its
> kind, two of every kind *shall come to you* to keep them
> alive. As for you, take for yourself some of all food which
> is edible, and gather it . . . and it shall be for food for you
> and them. (Gen. 6:20-21, emphasis added)

First God says that the animals will come to Noah (and how
will they come to Noah, if not by the command of God himself?).
Then God directs Noah to "take" the food himself (the food
won't come to him).

Noah's experience is the second time the Bible speaks of God gathering the animals (the first time was in the Garden of Eden when God brought the animals to Adam to be named).

After living together in the ark for a little over one year (377 days), Noah and the animals left the ark.

> So Noah went out with his sons and his wife and his sons' wives. And every animal, every creeping thing, and every bird, everything that moves on the earth, went out of the ark by families. (Gen 8:18-19 NRSV)

We are not told exactly what happened after the animals left the ark, but we can infer that God communicated to the animals how to behave for years after the Flood. In order to survive, animals had to coexist outside of the ark until there was enough time for them to reproduce in numbers enough to again populate the earth. As we discussed in chapter 4, this may mean that for a while animals were vegetarians.

If the animals had preyed on each other immediately there would not have been enough of them to populate the world. This is easy to see by considering that the gestation period for some animals is longer even than that of a human. Animals such as cows, deer, horses and elephants only have one offspring at a time, or very rarely two. Many animals cannot bear young until they reach at least two years of age, some even older. At that rate, it would have taken many years to repopulate earth. This strongly suggests that for a while after the Flood, God controlled the behavior and interactions of animals.

To further help the animals survive, God communicated to them again by putting the fear of man in them. God told Noah that the animals would now fear him:

> The fear and dread of you shall rest on every animal of
> the earth, and on every bird of the air, on everything that
> creeps on the ground, and on all the fish of the sea; into
> your hand they are delivered. (Gen. 9:2 NRSV)

God did this to help the animals survive, because in
delivering them to Noah God was giving people permission to
use animals as food.

The fact that the Bible mentions that God put the fear of
humans into the animals means that it was a significant event.
Yet it does not tell us that God had taken that same fear away in
order for the animals to come to Noah in the ark. This suggests
that perhaps animals did not fear humans prior to the end of
the Flood.

Many years later, the prophet Isaiah mentioned animals when
he prophesied about a time in the future when the Messiah
would return to this earth and set up his rule:

> The wolf shall live with the lamb, the leopard shall lie
> down with the kid, the calf and the lion and the fatling
> together, and a little child shall lead them. The cow and
> the bear shall graze, their young shall lie down together;
> and the lion shall eat straw like the ox. The nursing child
> shall play over the hole of the asp, and the weaned child
> shall put its hand on the adder's den. They will not hurt
> or destroy in all my holy mountain; for the earth will be
> full of the knowledge of the LORD as the waters cover the
> sea. (Is. 11:6-9 NRSV)

One of the most overlooked miracles involving an animal
occurred when Jesus rode a donkey into Jerusalem on Palm
Sunday. Jesus told two of his disciples,

Go into the village opposite you, and . . . you will find
a colt tied there, on which no one yet has ever sat; untie
it and bring it here. If anyone says to you, 'Why are
you doing this?' you say, 'The Lord has need of it;' and
immediately he will send it back here. (Mark 11:2-3)

Anyone who has ever tried to ride an unbroken horse, donkey
or ox, knows firsthand that they cannot be easily ridden. A person
only needs to read a book or see a movie about America's Old
West, or watch a rodeo, to witness how difficult it is to ride an
unbroken animal. Yet that is what Jesus did.

He took a colt that had never been ridden and rode it peacefully through Jerusalem. The colt went in the correct direction, at
the right speed. Besides the miracle of riding the colt, controlling
the colt was another miracle. Once an equine or bovine is broken
to the point where it can be handled, it must then be taught the
signals for control, speed, and direction.

On top of these miracles, there was yet another. The donkey
did not panic when the crowds shouted and laid their coats
and palm branches in the road before Jesus. Even many trained
animals cannot handle the type of noise and activity that surrounded the donkey colt that day on the road to Jerusalem.
Consider the police horses used in large cities today. The horses
must have a certain temperament to qualify for this type of
work. Some are too nervous and jumpy to handle the crowds and
noise. Yet this untrained donkey colt walked calmly through it
all, carrying the Messiah. This is another demonstration of God's
communication with and control over all animals.

Even though we do not understand how God communicates with animals, the Bible shows us that he has communicated with animals from the beginning, in the Garden of
Eden, and throughout earth's history. According to the Bible,

he will continue to do so in the future.

Today, God answers the prayers of humans; he is not a silent God. He has given us the Bible as his personal letter. God also communicates with us in many other ways if we are quiet enough to listen. Why then would he not be in touch with the rest of his creation?

Isaiah points out that God will communicate with the animals, directing them to behave in the same way as they did in the Garden of Eden. This passage also says that the animals will have full knowledge of the Lord, or an understanding of the plan of God. We are told that the "earth shall be full of the knowledge of the Lord." The term "earth" means everything on the planet, not just humans.[2] The behavior of animals will be changed during this time; by God's orders, they will not act the way they did in the past. They will change their lifestyle in obedience to God's directive.

In another well-known instance, God ordered a great fish to swallow Jonah. We do not know if this fish existed previously or was created for this purpose; however, the term "appointed" implies that the fish existed and obeyed God.

The Lord appointed a great fish to swallow Jonah, and Jonah was in the stomach of the fish three days and three nights. (Jonah 1:17)

A few cases in recent history of people being swallowed whole by sharks and surviving provide modern examples to support the truth of Jonah's story.

10
ANIMALS AS AGENTS OF GOD'S JUDGMENT

THERE ARE MANY instances in the Bible of God using animals and insects to punish people. Sometimes the event is used as a harsh means to persuade people to obey God's directions. What can we learn from that? If a dog bites a human, or one animal kills another, does that mean that God is using the animal to punish the human or the other animal? Would God, who is able to do anything he wants, need to use animals at all?

In the book of Exodus, God commanded Moses to use bugs to punish the Egyptians for holding the Israelites captive:

> Then the LORD said to Moses, 'Say to Aaron, "Stretch out your staff and strike the dust of the earth, so that it may become gnats throughout the whole land of Egypt."' And they did so; Aaron stretched out his hand with his staff and struck the dust of the earth, and gnats came on humans and animals alike; all the dust of the earth turned into gnats throughout the whole land of Egypt. (Ex. 8: 16-17 NRSV)

This may mean that the gnats were specially created out of the dust just for this event; or the gnats were as numerous as the dust of the desert; or perhaps the gnats were in the dust and came out. It might also refer to mosquitoes. Whether the insects were specially created or just unusually numerous and concentrated, God chose to use them to punish the Egyptians.[1]

Another example of animals meting out God's punishment occurs in the book of Leviticus. This book of laws was a manual for the Levites, the priests of the Israelites. God promised the Israelites that if they followed the law, he would provide rain and good harvest, and would keep their enemies at bay. God also told the Israelites that if they did not obey the laws, he would withhold the rain, causing famine and death. The drought would cause the wild animals to suffer as well, and God warned:

> I will let loose the wild beasts among you, which shall
> rob you of your children, and destroy your cattle, and
> make you few in number, so that your ways shall become
> desolate. (Lev. 26:22 NRSV)

This implies that the beasts are otherwise kept under control.

The book of Numbers recounts how God used snakes to punish the Israelites' lack of faith and gratitude. While the Israelites were wandering in the desert, Moses decided to change their route to a longer one. The people got angry and frustrated. They complained about the change in plans, the living conditions and the food (manna) that God provided for them to eat. As a result of all of the complaining, God became angry and caused poisonous snakes to bite and kill many of the Israelites.

> And the Lord sent fiery serpents among the people and
> they bit the people, so that many people of Israel died.
> (Num. 21:6)

God also used hornets to protect and fight for the Israelites:

And I sent the hornet before you, which drove out before
you the two kings of the Amorites; it was not by your
sword or by your bow. (Josh. 24:12 NRSV)

This passage may be taken literally, which would mean that
God used hornets to chase away the armies of Israel's enemies.
The hornets might also refer to the Egyptian army that raided
the Canaanites on a regular basis, weakening them for the Israelites. Or it might mean that God put the fear of the Israelites
into their enemies and they ran away in a panic, like a swarm of
hornets. I believe, though, that this passage means God literally
sent hornets to drive the armies away. God specifically says that
he sent the hornets *before* the Israelites. And the word used in the
Bible for hornet is considered to mean the literal insect. This type
of stinging hornet can still be found in the Middle East. Also, the
text says that it was "not by your sword or bow," stating that it
was not an act of the soldiers that drove away their enemies.

In another example, Isaiah prophesies that Edom will be
destroyed. The wild animals that normally do not live in a city
will possess this land at the command of God.

There shall the owl nest and lay and hatch and brood in
its shadow; there too the buzzards shall gather, each one
with its mate. . . . For the mouth of the Lord has commanded, and his spirit has gathered them. (Is. 34:15-16
NRSV)[2]

Further, the book of the prophet Joel refers to a special plague
that had come over the land, that is recorded in history. This
plague was so unique that Joel says it will be remembered from
generation to generation. Joel uses the plague as an example of
the judgments of God that are to come in the last days, which

will include the tribulation, the millennial reign of Christ, and beginnings of the new heavens and new earth (*See* Rev. 6-20; 2 Pet. 3:10-13). Again, this Scripture gives us an example of God directing his creatures for his purposes:

> What the cutting locust left, the swarming locust has eaten. What the swarming locust left, the hopping locust has eaten, and what the hopping locust left, the destroying locust has eaten. (Joel 1:4 NRSV)

This is not a case of four attacks by the same kind of locust, but actually four different types of locust which is what makes this swarm so unique.

Then God gives his promise of forgiveness and restoration. It is interesting to note that because the land and animals suffer from the plague, they are included in the promise of better times.

> Do not fear, O land, rejoice and be glad, for the Lord has done great things. Do not fear, beasts of the field, for the pastures of the wilderness have turned green, for the tree has borne its fruit, the fig tree and the vine have yielded in full. So rejoice, O sons of Zion, and be glad in the Lord your God; for He has given you the early rain for your vindication. And He has poured down for you the rain. (Joel 2:21-23)

Note that here Joel mentions the land, then the animals, and then humans—all three specifically and in the order of creation.

1 Kings 13 tells how God punished a disobedient prophet by having a lion kill him. The circumstances surrounding this punishment indicate that the lion was under God's direct command.

In this account, a young prophet of the Lord spoke his prophecy in public, accompanied by miracles. The word of his message would have spread quickly. Next he followed God's directions and delivered God's message to the wicked King Jeroboam. After he finished, the young prophet was told by God to go right home using a different route than the one by which he arrived. Meanwhile an old prophet who lived in the city had heard about the arrival of the young prophet. He invited the young prophet to visit and spend time with him. But as instructed by God, the young prophet refused and continued on his way home.

The old prophet must have been very lonely. He decided to tell the young prophet that an angel of the Lord had instructed him to give the young man a message. He told him that God had changed his mind, and the young prophet should forget his earlier instructions and visit with the old prophet. As a result, the young prophet disobeyed his direct instructions from God and went to visit the old prophet.

God became angry and killed the younger prophet while he traveled home. The old prophet who lied to the younger prophet, causing him to disobey God, heard of the young man's death and went to see for himself what had happened.

When the old prophet found the body of the young prophet, he saw the lion standing over the man's body, next to his donkey. This was an unusual act and a miracle for several reasons: 1) the lion did not maul the body of the human; 2) the lion did not touch the donkey; 3) the donkey stood quietly next to the lion and a dead body; and 4) lions were uncommon, although not unheard of, in that area.

This was a sign that the punishment was directly from God, since this behavior was out of character for both the lion and the donkey. If God had simply struck the prophet dead, it would not have been unusual, since people died suddenly then as they do today.[3]

The Bible does show us that God directs and controls all his creation, using whatever means he chooses, to get our attention.

However, do not think that every time an animal kills someone, it is divine punishment. As we discussed in chapter 4, animals and humans are allowed to kill for food. According to biblical accounts, we can determine if an animal is acting under divine influence when the animal does not follow the normal behavior of its kind. So the animal who bites its owner is not acting on the orders of God. There are many reasons why this can happen, but it is within the range of what is considered justifiable behavior.

It is only when the behavior and circumstances of an animal are not normal for that animal, that the behavior could be a directive from God.

11
CAN ANIMALS BE EVIL?

I HAVE WORKED with some dogs that had a fearsome, evil look in their eyes—a look that made me feel uncomfortable, even though rehabilitating such dogs has been my job for many years. Could these dogs be evil? Could an animal be possessed by an evil spirit, a satanic demon?

Sometimes a beloved pet dog attacks a family member and the owner comes to me for help. The family feels betrayed and very hurt. Sometimes they feel that the attack is personal and will ask me if their dog is evil. In this chapter we will explore the concepts of evil and sin and how they relate to animals. Are any animals really evil? What does the Bible say about this?

In order to answer this question we must understand what evil means. Then we can look at how the events recorded in the Bible show us the way evil works, where it comes from and when it involves animals.

Webster's New World Dictionary defines evil as immoral conduct, or conduct causing pain or harm. This implies a willful, premeditated act. It would be an act that originates either from the acting individual or from an evil spiritual being acting through the individual.

A Christian view of evil falls into two categories: physical evil and moral evil. In general, evil is greater than sin. Evil combines the act with the consequences.

Physical evil is very simply explained: when humans violate the basic rules of God, they experience the repercussions for what they did. Moral evil comes from humankind's sinful nature. Behind all of this is the spiritual battle between God and his angels and Satan and his demons.

It will also help if we understand the Christian view of sin. The Bible tells us that sin existed before the Fall of humankind in the Garden of Eden. However, the sin that occurred at that time was the desire on the part of Adam and Eve to be like God. They desired to be independent from God. This was a God-denying aspiration on the part of Adam and Eve, and the actual act of disobedience (eating of the forbidden fruit) was an expression of this aspiration.

Pretend that you are a fly sitting in the Garden of Eden, watching what is about to unfold in the third chapter of Genesis. Eve is working in the garden as God has directed her to do. As has happened before, she feels drawn to the forbidden tree. Perhaps she makes excuses to be in that part of the Garden: she wants to pick berries, for example. As Eve approaches the berry bushes, she hears:

"Psssssst, pssssst. Hey, Eve."

"Who's that?"

"Eve, over here."

"Come out where I can see you!"

At her invitation, a beautiful serpent walks out from under the large leaf where he has been waiting.

"Hello, serpent, how are you today?"

"Oh I'm fine. I see that you are back again looking at the forbidden tree."

Eve does not comment.

"Eve, you keep coming here; I see you all the time."

"I know." She pauses. "The tree is so beautiful and

the luscious-looking fruit is always ripe." Another pause; then she asks, "Why are you here?"

Ignoring her question, the serpent replies, "Why don't you eat the fruit from that tree?"

"Because God said if we eat the fruit we will die."

We all know what happened next, but in order for us to see whether or not the serpent was evil we have to understand exactly what transpired. First, the serpent did not make Eve sin. Eve let the serpent talk her into eating the fruit, and then she convinced Adam to eat the fruit as well. In Eve's heart, she wanted to eat the fruit. First she harbored the desire. Like any sin, Eve had to allow it into her life. The serpent could not force her to sin, but the serpent could push her over the edge with argument and temptation (people will make excuses to justify sin). When Eve realized that the serpent was questioning God's orders not to eat from that tree, she could have rebuked the serpent and refused to listen to it. Instead she continued her interaction with the serpent.

The serpent's temptation of Eve was a willful premeditated act. I imagine the serpent was waiting for Eve to come, knowing what it planned to do. Throughout the Bible we are taught that Satan looks for every possible way to make humans rebel against the rules God has established, and to disbelieve God and his message of salvation. Therefore we can see that in this case the serpent was evil.

But some may question whether or not this was a real serpent. Does the Bible tell us this was a real serpent, or Satan in the form of a serpent?

Now the serpent was more subtle and crafty than any living creature of the field which the Lord God had made. (Gen. 3:1 AMP)

First, the Bible calls it a serpent. Second, it gives us a description of the serpent's character—subtle and crafty. Subtle means not open, not direct, or not easy to detect. It means sly and not obvious. Crafty is another word for subtle. But crafty may also mean powerful, deceitful, and artful. We are told that the serpent was not only deceitful, but that it was good at deceiving.

The statement, "more subtle and crafty than any living creature of the field," compares the serpent to the rest of the animal kingdom. I believe that it speaks of a literal serpent. Think about it, why would God compare Satan to animals?

A number of biblical scholars believe this was an actual serpent, and not Satan disguising himself in the form of the serpent. In The Amplified Bible, the next sentence says, "And he [Satan] said to the woman . . ." Does this mean that Satan was using the serpent as a vehicle to talk to Eve, or that Satan showed himself to Eve in the form of a serpent?

And the huge dragon was cast down and out—that age-old serpent, who is called the Devil and Satan, he who is the seducer (deceiver) of all humanity the world over; he was forced out and down to the earth, and his angels were flung out along with him. (Rev. 12:9 AMP)

We know that in his original created form, Satan or Lucifer appeared as the most beautiful of angels. God describes Satan's beauty and perfection in Ezekiel 28:11-19. Satan was from the order of angels called Cherubim, and was given a special place of prominence guarding the throne of God. No other angelic beings are described as having the beauty, position and wisdom of Lucifer. He did not look like a serpent. The Ryrie Bible notes for this passage state that the serpent was "apparently a beautiful creature, in its uncursed state, that Satan used in the temptation."

According to Ryrie, Satan used an actual serpent, instead of appearing in the form of a serpent. Since the beautiful serpent allowed Satan to use him as a vehicle to talk to Eve, God cursed the serpent.[1]

> The Lord God said to the serpent, 'Because you have done this, cursed are you above all cattle, and above all wild animals; upon your belly you shall go, and dust you shall eat all the days of your life.' (Gen. 3:14)[2]

Note that God specifically said that the serpent is cursed *more than* (above) all other animals. God also cursed the ground, allowing weeds to hinder Adam's farming efforts. The physical appearance of the serpent was changed from a creature that walked with legs to one that now had to travel on its belly.

God's curse was for the living creature that was and is the serpent.

By transforming the serpent into its present form, God gave us a constant reminder of the Fall of Adam and Eve, which resulted in separation from God and caused the physical and spiritual death of all humans. God cursed the serpent above all cattle (domestic animals) and all wild animals. If the Bible were not talking about a literal serpent, why would God refer for the second time, to all of the animals of creation?

Some may ask why, at this point, God did not curse Satan instead of the serpent. God did not curse Satan because he was cursed already at some point in the past. He had been cast out of heaven with no hope of redemption.

The serpent allowed Satan to enter him and use him, which is why God cursed that serpent and all serpents.[3]

So far we have seen that at least one real, living creature, the serpent, was evil. But what about the rest of the animals on earth?

The Bible tells us about another situation where demons entered animals. Matthew chapter 8 records how Jesus encountered two men who were demon possessed and very violent. When they saw Jesus, the demons recognized him as the Son of God. They were afraid that Jesus was going to lock them in hell, and begged him instead to send them into a herd of swine. With this request the demons clearly acknowledged Jesus' authority.

> And behold, they shrieked and screamed, 'What have You to do with us, Jesus, Son of God? Have You come to torment us before the appointed time?' . . . The demons begged him, 'If you cast us out, send us into the herd of swine.' And he said to them, 'Go.' So they came out and entered the swine; and suddenly, the whole herd rushed down the steep bank into the sea and perished in the water. (Matt. 8:29 AMP, vss. 31-32 NRSV)

The demons were very upset and afraid; they shrieked and screamed. Yet what did this do to the swine? According to this account, the swine had no say or choice about being possessed by demons. Also, this indicated that the two men were possessed by many demons, enough to take over a whole herd of swine. By possessing the swine the demons destroyed them.

Does this mean that the swine were evil? Not at all, because unlike the serpent in the Garden of Eden, the swine did not give the demons permission to enter them. The serpent, on the other hand, did allow Satan to use it. This is indicated by the fact that all serpents suffer from the special curse of God, given in the Garden of Eden. The Bible does not state at all that those swine or any swine thereafter are cursed. The physical characteristics of swine were not changed, and Jesus spoke no criticism of them.

However, the curse on creation and the additional curse on

the serpent show us that all animals suffer from the Fall of humans into sin.

When humans sinned, all of creation was cursed and we have explained why, but that does not solve the question, why were all serpents cursed? Does the fact that the serpent allowed Satan to use it imply that all of God's creatures have free will? This may be one of the mysteries that will remain unanswered.

Ezekiel chapter 14 recounts how certain elders or spiritual leaders came to the prophet Ezekiel. They wanted to know about the future of Jerusalem. Ezekiel replied:

> For thus says the Lord God: 'How much more when I send My four severe judgments against Jerusalem: sword, famine, wild beasts, and plague to cut off man and beast from it!' (Ez. 14:21)

Various translations of this verse use the terms "evil" or "savage" for wild beasts. What does that mean?

In the book of Revelation more references are made to punishment by sword, famine, pestilence and by "the wild beasts of the earth" (Rev. 6:8). This would indicate that the beasts are not evil, but are obeying God by following his directive. To understand this part of biblical events, we can look to a more modern example.

Throughout history, most accounts of animals killing and eating humans have shown us that there has been a reason for it.

In their natural state in normal circumstances, wild animals do not prefer to kill and eat humans. All wild animals have a natural fear of humans which God put into them after the Flood. However, in some circumstances wild animals have been known to overcome this fear. For example, around the turn of the 19th century, the villages in the Himalayas of northern India were plagued by man-eating tigers. The tigers would drag off people and cattle, causing terror in those communities. The district officials turned to Lieutenant-Colonel Jim Corbett, a famous hunter, to rid the area of its man-eaters. Jim Corbett states in his book, *Man-Eaters of Kumaon,*

> As many of the stories in this book are about man-eating tigers, it is perhaps desirable to explain why these animals develop man-eating tendencies. A man-eating tiger is a tiger that has been compelled through the stress of circumstances beyond its control, to adopt a diet alien to it. The stress of circumstances is, in nine cases out of ten, wounds, and in the tenth case old age.

With this in mind, look again at Ezekiel 14:21 (above) which states, "sword, famine, pestilence, and evil or wild beasts." The famine and pestilence would kill the natural prey of the meat-eating animals. It would also weaken people, making them easy prey. This agrees with the experiences of Jim Corbett who observed that the wild animals resorted to killing and eating humans or eating the bodies of dead humans in order to survive.

Another similar situation occurred with the man-eating lions of Tsavo. In 1898, a pair of male lions terrorized the workers of the Uganda Railway for over nine months while they built the Tsavo River Bridge in East Africa. The lions killed and ate over 140 workers before they themselves were finally killed. While we will never know just why these specific lions became man-eaters, some interesting facts emerged.

In the 1890s, there was an outbreak of Rinderpest disease that killed millions of zebras, gazelles, and other wildlife. The number of attacks on humans by big cats increased across the continent at that time. Also, the burial practices for the workers at Tsavo were very poor. In some cases the men were not buried at all. This could have given the lions their first meal of human flesh, teaching them that humans were easy prey.

These examples of animals killing and eating humans show that in the isolated cases where God directs a lion to kill someone, such as the disobedient friend and the young prophet mentioned in the previous chapter, the animal is obeying God's orders; it is not in the nature of the beast to kill people under normal circumstances. In these cases, as far as we know, the lions were not starving, sick or otherwise unhealthy. All other instances in the Bible show us that the animals behaved according to the laws of nature, as demonstrated by Jim Corbett's tigers or the Tsavo lions.

In the Bible, the wild beasts killing and eating starving humans could be a form of punishment for the people. Although animals eating humans is repulsive to us, and not the food of choice for animals, it is food for the animals. In this situation, it seems as though the humans are the ones suffering the most, both physically and psychologically.

What we learn from the Bible is that except for the individual serpent in the Garden of Eden, there is no indication that animals are evil. There is no indication that animals purposely act out the will of Satan, although they do obey the orders of God. Does this mean that animals have free will to either obey or disobey God? We may only learn the answer to that question in heaven, when we can ask God ourselves. However, the Bible gives us much to think about.

12
ANIMALS MINISTER TO HUMANS

ONE TIME I CAUGHT a severe case of the flu; I had a high fever
and could not get out of bed for about three days. All during that
time, my cat would not leave my side. Day and night, she lay next
to me. If I reached out to pet her, she would purr and gently kiss
my forehead. She would only leave to eat and relieve herself, and
then she would immediately come back and stay with me. This
was unusual behavior for her since her days normally consisted of
sleeping in her favorite places, playing with the dog, watching the
wild birds at the bird feeder and sunning herself in a window. As
soon as I was well again, she resumed her regular routine.

Many pet owners have similar stories about how their pets
comforted them in times of need. Does the Bible say anything
about animals ministering to humans?

People have always kept animals to help them with various
tasks. We know that the livestock-guarding dogs originated
in the Middle East. By the time of Christ they were widely
employed by shepherds. The book of Job, which is considered to
be the oldest book of the Bible, makes reference to sheep dogs.

But now those younger than I mock me, Whose fathers I
disdained to put with the dogs of my flock. (Job 30:1)

This passage most likely refers to livestock-guarding dogs,
which were employed long before herding dogs.

Archaeologists have found an interesting description of life in the area of Canaan between 1971 and 1928 B.C., authored by an Egyptian named Sinuhe. In this account Sinuhe mentions that his hunting dogs helped provide some of the game for his meals—much the same as bird dogs are used today. We also know that animals of all kinds were kept as pets. Consider this example from the book of Second Samuel:

> But the poor man had nothing but one little ewe lamb which he had bought and brought up, and it grew up with him and his children. It ate of his own morsel, drank from his own cup, lay in his bosom, and was like a daughter to him. (2 Sam. 12:3 AMP)

While this depiction of a pet lamb, loved dearly by the man and his children, is a fictitious account told by the prophet Nathan to King David to illustrate a point, it was a circumstance that did not surprise David. Obviously it was not an uncommon thing to make a pet of an animal.

The New Testament also mentions keeping dogs as pets. For example, a Canaanite woman begging Jesus to heal her daughter of demon possession used this metaphor to persuade him:

> Even the dogs feed on the crumbs which fall from their master's table. (Matt. 15: 27)

The Amplified Bible reads: "Even the little pups eat the crumbs that fall from their master's table." These would be dogs kept in the house as pets, not the wild dogs that roamed the streets.

Today we understand the dynamics of pet therapy, that interacting with an animal in a positive manner can lower blood pressure, help people get rid of depression, ease loneliness, and help reach children who are mentally disturbed. Even though they may not have known it, the benefits to the ancient peoples were the same as they are now. This is one way that animals ministered to people in times past.

Despite the fact that many people during biblical times considered dogs unclean (God had told them that animals which walked on paws and ate carrion and blood were unclean to eat), the Bible does indicate that some Jewish people kept dogs and other animals as pets. However, there were also wild scavenging dogs that roamed the streets of towns and villages at night. It is not unreasonable to assume that many people acted in a hostile manner toward the wild dogs, throwing stones at them and chasing them away. Still, the gospel of Luke gives an example of these wild dogs actually ministering to the needs of a poor man.

> And at his gate lay a poor man named Lazarus, covered with sores, who longed to satisfy his hunger with what fell from the rich man's table; even the dogs would come and lick his sores. (Luke 16:20-21 NRSV)

Jesus used this example in a parable. He typically used parables, or stories, about things that his listeners could relate to, things that were commonplace in their lives.

Many people might read this and think, how terrible to have dogs lick sores. Yet consider the situation. The man sits by the gate of the city begging. The ground is dry and dusty. The dust contains the dung and garbage of many animals and people. The man has no one to come and wash his sores, and no means to clean himself.

Anyone who has ever seen a dog lick its own or another's sores or injuries will notice that it is done in a very healing way.

The dog licks gently in order to thoroughly cleanse the wound. We know today that a dog's mouth has fewer germs and bacteria than a human's mouth. The act of licking a wound is healing. So in reality, a dog licking the man's sores would keep the sores clean and promote healing.

In chapter 9, "God Communicates with Animals," we saw that animals ministered to a human when ravens fed Elijah.

History is filled with stories about people's affection toward animals, even the animals that help them with their jobs. Alexander the Great's love for his horse Bucephalus is well known. He named Bucephala, a city, after his horse.

Animals minister to people every day by providing company when they are alone. People often talk to their pets. Some people find joy in watching the wild birds, as is evident by the fact that there is an entire industry built around feeding and watching them.

The number of photographs and paintings that depict animals, both domestic and wild, attest to the pleasure they give to people. Although this is an indirect method, these animals are ministering to the needs of people.

One only has to watch a child cling to a stuffed toy to see how a representative of an animal meets their needs. Even more beautiful is the relationship between a child and a pet, whether it is a dog, cat, bird, horse or even one of many farm animals.

If you have had an animal curl up next to you for a quiet nap, you can attest to the comfort and joy it brings.

Consider this: No matter how a person looks, or what he has done or not done, regardless of any aspect of that person's life, an animal will love him unconditionally, never expecting anything in return. Isn't this the same type of unconditional love that God gives to us? Could this be a subtle lesson of love that God graciously gives us through our pets?

What a wonderful gift God has given us in creation, and especially in the many ways he allows animals to minister to us.

13
IS THE BIBLE UNCOMPLIMENTARY TO ANIMALS?

SOME PEOPLE COMPLAIN that the Bible does not have nice things to say about animals, and dogs in particular. So let's look at a few seemingly uncomplimentary passages and see what we find.

> Like a dog that returns to its vomit is a fool who repeats his folly. (Prov. 26:11)

People find this Bible verse distasteful. It illustrates that as sure as a dog will return to his vomit, a fool will be a fool again. Dogs eating their vomit must have been as disgusting during biblical times as it is to us today. However, when we understand why dogs do this, this behavior is not as bad as it sounds.

Dogs, and other canids such as wolves, do this because it is home cooking to them; they will return to their vomit up until a certain point of digestion. This is no different from a human mother pre-chewing food for a baby before canned baby food was invented. Keep in mind that in humans, digestion starts with the chewing of the food, so a baby's food must be mashed. With dogs, digestion takes place entirely in the stomach. They rip and tear their food until it is small enough to swallow, bolt it down and digest it in the stomach, without chewing it as humans do.

Therefore, in God's infinite wisdom, he allows the mother dog to ingest large amounts of food and, upon reaching her litter, regurgitate the food partly digested so that the young, with their weak baby teeth, can eat it. This takes place in the first stages of weaning the pups from milk to solid food. So when a dog vomits right after he has eaten, he will eat the food again. Once the food has been digested beyond a certain point, the dog will no longer return to the vomit.

A reference in the book of Isaiah characterizes dogs as dumb.

His watchmen are blind, all of them know nothing; all of them are dumb dogs unable to bark; dreaming, dreamers lying down, who love to slumber. (Is. 56:10-11)

The word "dumb" here doesn't mean "stupid" but "silent or mute," unable to talk or make sounds. Isaiah was warning the people that the professional prophets of the day were blind to the will of God, lazy, and unable to warn them of approaching danger.

This does not brand all dogs as mute or dumb, but only those who sleep and do not watch as they are supposed to. And yes, there are dogs that do not make good watchdogs. Apparently these dogs existed then as well as now.

So we see that the negative references to dogs in the Bible are not really negative at all, but are observations used to explain a point in a way that the reader can relate to.

The Bible often refers to horses in a positive manner, calling them brave and intelligent, as in Job 39:19-21:

Do you give the horse his might? Do you clothe his neck with a mane? Do you make him leap like the locust? His majestic snorting is terrible. He paws in the valley, and rejoices in his strength.

King Solomon admired lions so much that he had twelve

statues of lions on the steps to his home (1 Kings 12: 19-20). The lion was considered the king of the beasts; its strength is described and used in a promise in Micah 5:8-9:

Like a lion among the beasts of the forest, like a young lion among flocks of sheep, which, if he passes through, tramples down and tears, and there is none to rescue. Your hand will be lifted up against your adversaries, and all your enemies will be cut off.

Psalm 104:12 joyously describes the bird life:

Besides them [the springs in the valleys] the birds of the heavens dwell; they lift up their voices among the branches.

God loves his animal kingdom so much that he uses them to describe his own qualities. A reference to God's might and power is found in the book of Revelation. The Apostle John is weeping because for a moment, he is shown what it would be like without the sacrifice that Jesus made on the cross:

Then I began to weep greatly because no one was found worthy to open the book or to look into it; and one of the elders said to me, "Stop weeping; behold, the Lion that is from the tribe of Judah, the Root of David, has overcome so as to open the book and its seven seals." (Rev. 5:4-5)

This "Lion of Judah" is a reference to Jesus, a descendant of King David, who is from the tribe of Judah. On a gentler side, the Bible describes what happened after Jesus' baptism by John:

> Jesus came up immediately from the water; and behold,
> the heavens were opened, and he saw the Spirit of God
> descending as a dove and lighting on Him, and behold a
> voice out of the heavens said, 'This is My beloved Son, in
> whom I am well-pleased.' (Matt. 3:16-17)

So we see that the Holy Spirit chose to descend upon Jesus in the visible form of a dove.

You are probably familiar with the references to Jesus as a meek lamb or as "the lamb of God" to illustrate his humble nature.

The saving character of God is expressed in Exodus:

> Moses went up to God, and the Lord called to him from
> the mountain, saying, 'Thus you shall say to the house
> of Jacob and tell the sons of Israel: You yourselves have
> seen what I did to the Egyptians, and how I bore you on
> eagles' wings, and brought you to Myself.' (Ex. 19:3-4)

According to Walvoord and Zuck, when a mother eagle is teaching her young to fly, she will fly beneath them with outspread wings, so that they do not fall (pg. 138). So God is using the caring, protective nature of the eagle to demonstrate his protection for Israel. He is also illustrating his all-powerful nature.

Never lose sight of the fact that God loves all his creation. He said it was good. Some biblical references to animals are viewed as unpleasant by humans because they do not understand the nature of the animal behavior being described. But it is used as an example in the Bible because it is something that has happened for a long time and the people would be familiar with it. This does not mean it is bad. It is just a point of reference to describe a certain phenomenon. To explain his qualities God could have used examples from nature such as the power of a tornado or hurricane, or the gentleness of a warm spring breeze. But instead he chose to use the qualities of animals. I believe this is because he loves the animals and because we could relate to the examples and understand.

Consider that we humans do the same thing. Throughout history people have used the qualities of animals to describe human personalities and traits. Think of the terms, "sly like a fox," "stubborn as a mule," and "gentle as a dove."

14
WILL ANIMALS BE IN HEAVEN?

MANY PET OWNERS have expressed the same sentiment as Will Rogers when he said, "If there are no dogs in heaven, then when I die I want to go where they went."

Life without the beauty of God's creatures, even in heaven, does seem a bit empty. While the Bible does not speak directly to this concern, I believe it does give us some clues.

BIBLE THEMES

Let's review what we have learned about God's regard for animals.

God made all the rest of creation before he made humans; humans needed the created world in order to survive. The Bible teaches us that God loves everything he made, including animals.

When Adam and Eve sinned, God chose animals to represent his coming sacrifice on the cross. Of all the things that God created, of all the things he could have used, he chose animals for this purpose. God used animal sacrifice to show people that sin is destructive and causes death. Of course, animal sacrifice did not take away sin, but only covered it for one year; it would take a perfect sacrifice to get rid of sin forever. This perfect sacrifice was Jesus, the Christ. However, until Jesus came to earth, animals were God's chosen sacrifice.

When God decided to destroy the world in a flood, he had Noah build an ark to save his family and representatives of all the

creatures that would die in the Flood. God could have let all of
the animals die and then simply recreated them after the Flood.
If God hadn't wanted to save all the animals, Noah could have
built a much smaller ark. It would have taken less time and effort.
He would not have had to gather as much food. He would not
have had to take care of all those animals. But by saving the
animals, God showed Noah and all his descendants how much
he cares for animals.

Some people may believe that God had Noah save the animals
in order to provide food for Noah and his family. However, they
did not eat the animals while on the ark. It was only after the
Flood that God gave Noah permission to eat animals (*See* Gen. 9).
Besides, God did not need to save all those animals to provide food
for Noah. God could have sent Noah food in the same manner that
he gave the Israelites manna during the Exodus.

It is true that when God shows humans how much he cares
for and loves the animals, he is also demonstrating to humans
how much more he loves us.

> Look at the birds of the air, that they do not sow, nor
> do they reap nor gather into barns, and yet your heavenly
> Father feeds them. Are you not worth much more than
> they? . . . Observe how the lilies of the field grow; they do
> not toil nor do they spin, yet I say to you that not even
> Solomon in all his glory clothed himself like one of these.
> But if God so clothes the grass of the field, which is alive
> today and tomorrow is thrown into the furnace, will He
> not much more clothe you? (Matt. 6:26-30)

Jesus is telling us that he cares much more for us than he
does for the animals and the plants of the world. Yet look at how
much he cares for the animals. God loved his animals enough to

have Noah save them. Some people may argue that most of the animals perished in the Flood. Yes, that is true, but again, could there be an important message in this event?

> The Lord is not slow about His promise, as some count slowness, but is patient toward you, not wishing for any to perish but for all to come to repentance. (2 Pet. 3:9)

We see that it is the wish of God that all humankind should accept Jesus as their Savior and go to heaven. Yet just as most of the animals perished in the Flood, the Bible teaches us that many humans will not accept Jesus and will perish eternally in hell.

We cannot know for sure why God decided to kill all the animals and plants in a global flood. We are told that humans perished because they were so evil that they broke God's heart. So the death of the animals may have been a message that on Judgment Day many seemingly good people will be banished to hell for eternity; or it could have been a purely logistical issue. Noah could not have possibly built an ark large enough to house all the creatures of earth.

At Jesus' birth, the first beings on earth to see him, besides his parents, were the animals in the manger. When the shepherds on the hillside saw the angels and heard them proclaiming praises to God, the sheep also saw and heard this (*See* Luke 2:9-14). Remember that while the shepherds were afraid, the sheep did not stampede or show fear (think of Balaam's donkey). No mention is made of the reaction of the animals. Had there been chaos, one would expect the Bible to have noted it, and the shepherds would not then have left their flocks.

While the shepherds went to worship the newborn Christ, no harm came to the sheep. This could be by divine intervention or because the shepherds used livestock-guarding dogs (*See* chapter

12, "Animals Minister to Humans"). Some biblical scholars believe that the sheep in the pasture were the town of Bethlehem's Passover lambs. It would be fitting that the shepherds who were guarding the Passover lambs would be among the first to see Jesus, called the Lamb of God. If the lambs in the field were the Passover lambs, it would also make sense that they would be among the first to hear the announcement that it was the beginning of the end of the need for animal sacrifice.

Throughout the Bible the Messiah, Jesus, is referred to over and over as the Lamb of God. This refers to the sacrificial lamb. It is also a reference to the nature of a lamb: meek, mild, soft, trusting, innocent and obedient. These were all qualities of Jesus. He was led to the slaughter willingly, he died and his blood was shed for our sins.

The animal used on the Day of Atonement in the temple had to be without blemish. The main difference between Jesus' death and that of the lamb is that Jesus had to be punished for our sins. He was beaten, scorned, mocked, laughed at, tortured, and suffered for us. The animals that were killed as a sacrifice were killed in a humane, quick manner.

When Jesus rode into Jerusalem on the day that we now celebrate as Palm Sunday, he rode a donkey. He could have walked. He could have been carried on a litter by his friends. Instead he rode on a donkey. This showed that he had the right to claim the donkey as his own, and that he was entering the city as a king coming in peace, not as a military conqueror. This also gave a special honor to the animal.

All in all, the Bible does give us a sense of how important animals are to God.

A NEW CREATION

The Bible also gives us some direct clues about animals going to heaven. Let's start with King David, who is described as "a man after God's own heart." David was surrounded by the wickedness of the world. In order to survive, he would meditate on the faithfulness, righteousness and justice of God. David wrote about the blessings that humans and animals receive from him.

Your righteousness is like the mighty mountains, your judgments are like the great deep; you save humans and animals alike, O Lord. (Ps. 36:6 NRSV)

David could either mean that God saves the life of beasts on earth, or that God saves them from eternal death and extinction. However, if we look at the whole psalm, we see that David's focus is on God's gift of total salvation of the human soul. The psalm does not deal with survival on earth.

Romans 8:21-22 makes it clear that all of creation—earth and everything on it, everything in the universe, everything that God created—groans, waiting for the coming of Christ.

At that time, creation itself will be set free from corruption into the freedom of the glory of the children of God. For we know that the whole creation groans and suffers the pains of childbirth together until now. (Rom. 8:22)

Would the Bible tell us that all creation waits for something it has no knowledge of, or that will not happen? Or that it will not benefit from? This must mean that God will transform all his creation into the new world that he promised us will happen at the second coming of Christ, on the great Resurrection Day. So we see that God has included all his creation in his future plans.

DO ANIMALS HAVE A SPIRIT OR SOUL?

The main stumbling point for many people about animals going to heaven, is whether or not animals have spirits and/or souls. So we need to define these terms. The words "soul" and "spirit" are sometimes used interchangeably by Bible teachers and commentators.[1,2] Yet all agree that there are two different entities here.

> For the word of God is living and active and sharper than any two-edged sword, and piercing as far as *the division of soul and spirit*, of both joints and marrow, and able to judge the thoughts and intentions of the heart. (Heb. 4:12, emphasis added)

For purposes of this discussion, we will use "spirit" to describe the quality possessed by every living creature. This includes angels and other spiritual beings. According to *Nave's Topical Bible*, the spirit is

> that in the immaterial part of man which is related to worship, communion with God and Divine influence. It is distinguished from the body and the soul. (pg. 1207)

We will use the word "soul" to describe what is only possessed by people. It is part of what makes each one of us unique. So one might say that the spirit is our connection with God and the soul connects the body with the spirit. Nave's explains the relationship between the spirit, body and soul this way:

> The body is the house of the soul, the instrument through which it relates to the material creation; the spirit gives the soul its consciousness of God. The soul is the seat of will, affections, personality. (pg. 1201)

In our current state, our body and entire being is driven by our soul; we are either worldly or, as described in the following Scripture, being "sanctified" or set apart from worldliness.

> Now may the God of peace Himself sanctify you entirely; and may your spirit and soul and body be preserved complete, without blame at the coming of our Lord Jesus Christ. (1 Thess. 5:23)

While this verse emphasizes the work God wants to do in us as whole persons, many Bible scholars have found significance in the Apostle Paul's mention of "spirit, soul, and body."

So what is the difference between humankind, who are created with both spirit and soul, and animals that have only a spirit? People, having a soul, need to be saved. Humans are sinners who have a chance to have eternal life.

> Whoever brings back a sinner from wandering will save the sinner's soul from death . . . For those who live according to the flesh set their minds on the things of the flesh, but those who live according to the Spirit set their minds on the things of the Spirit. To set the mind on the flesh is death, but to set the mind on the Spirit is life and peace. (James 5:20; Rom. 8:5-6 NRSV)

Since the Fall of Adam and Eve, all humans are born in sin, and thus not able to have the fellowship with their Creator that Adam had in the Garden. Only humans have a soul that needs to be saved from eternal separation from God.

Angels and other created beings in heaven are pure spirit; they do not need a soul because they do not have a physical body. They are either with God, and are angels, or they fell from grace with

God and are demons. Angels made their choice in the presence of
God. They do not have a second chance. They knew who God was
and who Satan was. They will exist for eternity, either as angels in
heaven or demons in hell.

As we have seen throughout this book, God communicates
with animals of earth, his creation. According to the explanation
in *Nave's Topical Bible* of what the spirit does, animals would need
a spirit to communicate with God. If animals have a spirit, where
will that spirit go when the animal dies?

In the New Testament book of James, we read:

> For just as the body without the spirit is dead, so also
> faith without works is dead. (James 2:26)

The reference to the body being dead means, obviously, physical death. So according to James, a body cannot physically live
without the spirit. Therefore all living animals must have a spirit.

Many times the Bible tells us that all of creation praises God,
acknowledges God and worships God. If the spirit is "that in the
immaterial part of man which is related to worship, communion
with God and Divine influence," then it would seem logical that,
if all of the animal kingdom worships God, animals too must
have a spirit.

With this thought let us look at what King Solomon has
to say about humans and beasts. Solomon said that no one
can demonstrate the difference between humans and beasts, that
death negates any difference between them.

> For that which befalls the sons of men befalls beasts; even
> [in the end] one thing befalls them both. As the one dies,
> so dies the other. Yes, they all have one breath and spirit, so
> that a man has no preeminence over a beast; for all is vanity

(emptiness, falsity, and futility)! . . . Who knows whether the human spirit goes upward and the spirit of animals goes downward to the earth? (Ecc. 3:19 AMP; 3:21 NRSV)

Was Solomon saying that animals have spirits or was he just pointing out that when humans and beasts die, they both turn to ashes and dust?

Why would Solomon ask this question, if he did not believe that animals have spirits? Keep in mind that according to 1 Kings 4:29-34, God gave Solomon more wisdom than anyone has had before or since. The passage states that Solomon was wise regarding all of creation, not just humans.

He spoke of trees, from the cedar that is in Lebanon even to the hyssop that grows on the wall; he spoke also of animals and birds and creeping things and fish. (1 Kings 4:33)

NOT CREATED IN GOD'S IMAGE

Only humans were created in the image of God. Historic, biblical Christianity recognizes that God is triune, comprised of the Father, the Son, and the Holy Spirit—three persons in one essence, three ways in which God has made himself known to us and in which he relates to us.

Similarly, humans are the only created beings in which there is found the threeness of body, soul and spirit (*See* 1 Thess. 5:23). We relate to God through our bodies, our souls, and our spirits. Our souls are what ennable us to make moral choices.

And put on the new self, which in the likeness of God has been created in righteousness and holiness. (Eph. 4:23-24)

Humans have the opportunity to be restored to the full image of God which has been distorted by sin. Even though animals do not have a soul, this does not exclude animals from heaven.

OTHER CREATURES IN HEAVEN BESIDES HUMANS

The Bible tells us that there are many different types of beings and creatures in heaven besides humans:

> And the first creature was like a lion, and the second creature like a calf, the third creature had a face like that of a man, and the fourth creature was like a flying eagle. And the four living creatures, each one of them having six wings, are full of eyes around and within; and day and night they do not cease to say, 'HOLY, HOLY, HOLY, is the LORD GOD, THE ALMIGHTY, who was and who is and who is to come!' (Rev. 4:7-8)

Later in Revelation we see that the creatures command the seals of judgment to come forth. So the creatures are not insignificant beings, but have a purpose and a job in heaven. These creatures are not like anything on earth. However, the book of Revelation also mentions horses a number of times.

> And I looked, and behold, a white horse, and he who sat on it had a bow; and a crown was given to him; and he went out conquering, and to conquer. (Rev. 6:2)

The Apostle John, writer of Revelation, states that one of the living creatures has the face of a man. This illustrates to us that heaven is not populated by humans and angels alone, but that other beings exist there as well; and at least some members of the animal kingdom as we know it, horses, will be there.

John goes on to tell us that the living creatures worship God along with the angels and the elders around the throne of God. That they all speak the same language is also evidenced in the dialog between them.

> Then I looked, and I heard the voice of many angels surrounding the throne and the living creatures and the elders; they numbered myriads of myriads and thousands of thousands, singing with full voice, 'Worthy is the Lamb that was slaughtered to receive power and wealth and wisdom and might and honor and glory and blessing!'
>
> Then I heard every creature in heaven and on earth and under the earth and in the sea, and all that is in them, singing, 'To the one seated on the throne and to the Lamb be blessing and honor and glory and might forever and ever!' And the four living creatures said, 'Amen!' And the elders fell down and worshiped. (Rev. 5:11-14 NRSV)

This passage makes it clear that all of God's creatures are in heaven worshiping God. *The Ryrie Study Bible* simply notes for verse 5:13, "All creation joins in praise to God and the Lamb."

Note that John's use of the one word "creatures" refers to all creatures in heaven and on earth and under the earth and in the sea. In the *New Bible Dictionary* the definition for creature emphasizes beings that are alive on earth rather than created beings in heaven. So we can assume that it means all created beings on earth will be in heaven. He is not talking about people alone.

So we see that God loves all of his creation and that there are beings in heaven that are neither human nor angels.

NOT CREATED TO BE IMMORTAL?

Many people believe that animals were not created to be

immortal. Let's review what the Bible says. Animals and all of
the earth were created before man. We do not know how long
Adam and Eve and the rest of creation lived before Adam and Eve
sinned. Up until that point, as far as we know, there was no death
on earth. Can we assume that, if Adam and Eve had not sinned, no
one would have died, not even animals? If sin had not entered the
world, would all of God's created beings have lived forever?

Let us look again at what the Bibles tells us about heaven.
Revelation 22:1 says that there will be a crystal-clear river having
the tree of life on either side, which bears a different fruit each
month. The Bible mentions the leaves of the tree, which are for
the healing of the nations. In addition, in John 14:2 Jesus tells of
many mansions in heaven.

In Revelation 21:9-27 John describes a glimpse of the New
Jerusalem. The city has the brilliance of clear jasper. It has a
high wall with twelve gates. There are twelve foundation stones.
The city is fifteen hundred miles long, wide and high. The
walls are made of jasper, the city pure gold. The foundation
stones are adorned with jasper, sapphire, chalcedony, emerald,
sardonyx, sardius, chrysolite, beryl, topaz, chrysoprase, jacinth
and amethyst. The gates are made of pearls, the streets of gold.
The glory of the Lord lights the city.

> He who has an ear, let him hear what the Spirit says to the
> churches. To him who overcomes, I will grant to eat of the
> tree of life which is in the Paradise of God. (Rev. 2:7)

There are two things to consider about this Bible passage.
First we are told directly by God that there are trees in heaven
and we can eat the fruit of those trees. Second is the use of the
word paradise. The word "paradise" is used three times in the Old
Testament. It may refer to a king's forest, a park, or an orchard.

It was understood that the word was used to describe a wonderful place and time of glory, identical with the Garden of Eden. A new "garden of God" in the world to come is pictured beautifully in the last chapters of Revelation.

We know that there are horses in heaven, as well as creatures that we have never seen. When we consider that many of the elements that are on this earth are also in heaven, and that heaven has a garden, why would God leave out the animals? Wouldn't eliminating any part of his creation from heaven imply that those elements of his creation were somehow less valued by God? Remember that, after God created the earth and all the creatures in it, he said it was very good. Although God values humans over all the rest of his creation, and only they are made in his image, he would not necessarily exclude the other creatures from heaven.

NOT EXCLUDED FROM HEAVEN

Finally, consider this: in all creation, only humans were disobedient to God. We are told in the Bible that the seas and wind obeyed Jesus when he rebuked them. All the heavenly bodies in the universe obey God by following the paths that he created for them. Even in spite of man's effect on the earth, everything in creation is in obedience to God. Only humans exist outside of the will of God, and even they are given the opportunity to go to heaven. In fact, Jesus said heaven is a place that is being prepared for his followers (*See* John 14:2).

Therefore, though we do not know for certain, the Bible gives us lots of clues. I believe because God said all his creation was good, including animals, that animals will be included in heaven. It does not seem logical that with all the other elements of the earth which are described as being in heaven, including plants and even specifically horses, the rest of the animal world should be left out—especially when the Bible says many times that the only beings who are not in heaven are people who do not accept Jesus as their Savior, Satan, and his demons. There is no mention of anything else being excluded from heaven.

ANIMALS FOR OUR ENJOYMENT

Finally, it seems to me, our loving God will want animals to be in heaven to add to our enjoyment. Heaven, after all, will be full of delights of all kinds much like we have here on this earth. But there won't be any sin. God delights in giving good gifts to his children (*See* Matt. 7:11). You have probably experienced the affection, loyalty, and playfulness of animals. In heaven we will be able to enjoy animals even more. And the animals themselves will be free of the distrust, abuse, misunderstanding, neglect, and death that are the effects of sin in this world.

15
CONCLUSION:
Lessons From The Animals

GOD'S CREATURES ARE not a major theme of his book. The Bible is not written for the sake of animals, although they are an important part of biblical history and theology. God has used animals to teach us a number of lessons.

The first death on earth was the death of an animal. The first death was also the first promise of an escape from eternal death; just as God killed an animal to cover Adam and Eve's nakedness, the shame of their sin, he would also send Jesus, whose death would completely remove the sin of all humankind. It was trading death for life. It demonstrated that only God could provide the means to escape the death of the human soul.

Adam, who had never killed anything, now had to kill animals as a sacrifice for the atonement of his sin. Over and over, as a reminder of the cost of sin, humans had to kill animals. With each death of an animal, humans were reminded that they could not save themselves.

To further bring home this point, God saved all the animal species along with Noah and his family. In this way God showed beyond a shadow of a doubt that he loved his creatures. Imagine how Noah and his family felt. Never having seen a flood, and perhaps never before having seen many of the animal species that came to him, Noah had to be awed by this dramatic event. It was obvious to Noah that there were more animals saved than people, and that God loved all the creatures in the ark. Could the act of saving the animals have been God's way of demonstrating that animals had a plan in eternity?

In Genesis 22 God asked Abraham to sacrifice his only son Isaac. In faith, Abraham prepared to do this. But at the last minute God stopped him and provided a ram to be sacrificed in Isaac's place. This dramatic event foreshadowed the sacrifice of God's only son, Jesus Christ. Abraham's experience was recorded as a message to humans. No matter how much faith Abraham had, it was a severe trial to be asked to plunge the knife into his only son. If it were not a difficult thing for Abraham to do, God would not have tested Abraham in this way. This incident showed Abraham—and shows us—that God himself would provide the sacrifice for humankind, just as he miraculously provided the ram for Abraham.

Animals were a part of God's miracles, lessons for people, and they received special blessings. It was a special honor for animals to be among the first to see the baby Jesus. This was part of God's plan; he could have provided an animal-free shelter for Mary and Joseph.

The author hopes this book has encouraged the reader to re-examine his or her beliefs. It is difficult to consider God's relationship with animals without considering God's nature, as well as our own personal relationship with God. We must each decide for ourselves: who is God, and what is our relationship to him? We must decide what we believe about life after death and how salvation works. We need to solidify our beliefs about our own body, soul and spirit. We cannot go where animals will be eternally if we do not know where we will go when we die.

If you are unsure about this, I urge you to search for the truth in the Bible, and consider what it says about the one true God, angels, the devil, heaven and hell. In doing so I hope you will find, as I have found, grace, hope, peace, and new life in Jesus Christ.

EPILOGUE:
The Creator's Free Gift

KNOWING HOW MUCH many of us would love the animals he created, God has used animals to teach us some important lessons about salvation:

1) In order to go to heaven we must accept Jesus as Savior.
2) Salvation is a gift; it is totally free and cannot be earned.
3) All we have to do is accept this gift.

God used Noah and the Flood to teach us valuable lessons. Although Noah's grandfather, Methuselah, and his father, Lamech, had died before the Flood, Noah may well have had living brothers, sisters, and other relatives. As Noah sat in the ark, he listened to the rain pelting the wood, heard the sounds of the rising water, and for a short while, he heard the cries of the people who were dying. Some were his relatives; some may have been people who were not so bad, just as there are kind, yet unsaved, people in the world today. Many were babies and young children. Yet those people perished then, just as those who do not accept Jesus as Lord, according to the Bible, will perish in eternity.

How blessed Noah and his family must have felt to be alive. They rejoiced as they experienced firsthand God's love for them, for humankind, and for animals. Undoubtedly, Noah understood that God was in control of this whole event. For the rest of his life, and the lives of his family for generations, the Flood had to be a major topic of thought and conversation. The amazement and fear of God was strong in them. It was very real. We can have the same assurance of God's loving care and certainty of our salvation that Noah had.

Throughout the Bible, God uses animals along with prophets, miracles and the teachings of Jesus and his disciples to get across his message of salvation to men and women.

> But God, being rich in mercy, because of His great
> love with which He loved us, even when we were dead in
> our transgressions, made us alive together with Christ (by
> grace you have been saved), and raised us up with Him,
> and seated us with Him in the heavenly places, in Christ
> Jesus, in order that in the ages to come He might show
> the surpassing riches of His grace in kindness toward us
> in Christ Jesus.
>
> For by grace you have been saved through faith; and
> that not of yourselves, it is the gift of God; not as a result
> of works, that no one should boast.
>
> For we are His workmanship, created in Christ Jesus
> for good works, which God prepared beforehand, that we
> should walk in them. (Eph. 2:4-10)

Let your love of animals lead you to love for their Creator and acceptance of his love for you.

NOTES

Chapter 1

1. The term "backyard bred" is used to identify those exotic animals which are bred purely for profit. Backyard breeders do not breed for health or purity, and often keep the animals in poor conditions bearing no resemblance to their natural habitat. They typically do not care if the animal makes a good pet or not since their goal is to make a profit off the public's desire to own unusual pets.

2. So many people believe that dogs are descended from wolves that I find it necessary to add the following information.

So far research shows that there is very little DNA variation between dogs and wolves.

Yet anyone who researches wolf behavior and dog behavior realizes that they are very different. With few exceptions, a pure wolf does not make a good pet. Wolves do not behave like our pet dogs even though they have some similar behavior traits. If the latest evidence in science is correct and humans did not domesticate dogs, how did this happen? Is it possible that God created subspecies within each group of animals and some are wild and some are domesticated, yet their DNA is similar?

3. Some people feel that the different breeds of animals are evidence of evolution. They point out all of the changes in plants and animals that have taken place throughout history. They assume that the changes are evidence of evolution, and that therefore the biblical account of creation is false. What they do not consider is that nowhere in the Bible does it say that humans cannot breed animals and change their characteristics to create variety. Nowhere is it written that what God has created has to stay exactly the same. It is simply a matter of fact that, no matter how much humans change the appearance and tweak the behavior of animals, the chemical make-up is the same. In essence, a dog is a dog, a cow a cow, and so forth. That changes have occurred since the beginning of the created world is evidenced by the fact that certain plant and animal species have become extinct. However, nothing new has been created or come into existence since then.

4. "Us" refers to the trinity of God.

5. When humans sinned against God in the Garden of Eden, they lost the salvation of their spirit and soul; they were separated from the

goodness and grace of God. The spirit is not the same as the soul. All beings, including animals, have a spirit.

Chapter 7

1. "Crabs: A Landmark Study" is a summary of another article, "Homing in the Swimming Crab Thalamita crenato: A Mechanism Based on Underwater Landmark Memory," Richard Milner, *Animal Behavior* issue 60, 2000.

2. Researchers are just discovering that animals have episodic memory, or the ability to recall details of the past and present and to think of the future. (*See* the April 03, 2007 *New York Times*, "Time in the Animal Mind," by Carl Zimmer.) Yet the Bible shows us that animals are capable of episodic memory and more.

Chapter 8

1. The Bible also makes it clear that ghosts are not part of God's plan either. Neither human nor animal ghosts roam the earth. "For the living know they will die; but the dead do not know anything, nor have they any longer a reward, for their memory is forgotten" (Ecc. 9:5).

This is not the only passage in the Bible that tell us that once a living thing dies, it is no longer involved in or a part of life on earth. According to the Bible, communication with the dead is a trick of Satan. But then the issue of ghosts is the topic for another whole book!

Chapter 9

1. The cognitive ability of animals, their ability to think, has been acknowledged by scientists for many years. According to Dr. Michael W. Fox, a recognized authority on canids, "They use foresight (the ability to set goals) and hindsight (learning from experience) in carefully thought-out behavior." Dr. Fox goes on to list the cognitive abilities of animals, including observational learning, symbolic behavior, imitative behavior, psychological disturbance, insightful behavior, reasoning, a sense of reciprocity, imagination, a sense of humor, and mind-reading. ("Understanding Your Pet," Michael W. Fox, *McCalls*, March 1984, pg. 80 & 120.)

2. "For the creation was subjected to futility, not willingly, but because of Him who subjected it, in hope that the creation itself also will be set free from its slavery to corruption into the freedom of the glory of the children of God. For we know that the whole creation groans and suffers the pains of childbirth together until now" (Rom. 8: 20-22).

This passage is, Charles Ryrie explains, "a statement of the Christian hope as it affects the individual (v.18) and the entire creation (vv. 19-25). After Adam sinned, God was obliged to subject the creation to futility so that man in his sinful state might retain some measure of dominion over creation. Nature was involved for evil in man's fall; she will be emancipated when man receives the adoption as sons" (pg. 1802).

Chapter 10

1. Since the priests of Egypt prided themselves in being clean, this plague mortified them by polluting their physical bodies. Also, an attack of this sort could have been an attack directed toward the Egyptian god Set, the god of the desert. The plague of insects would show the Egyptians that the God of the Hebrews is more powerful than their gods (Walvoord & Zuck, pg 122).

2. As we read Isaiah 34: 15-16, note that God says the Lord commanded and his spirit gathered them—demonstrating that animals do the bidding of God.

3. Some may wonder why God killed the young prophet who was deceived by the old prophet, instead of killing the old prophet. The reason is that the young prophet publicly declared the prophecy of God's judgment on Jeroboam. Many people, if not all of Israel would have heard this. God could not allow his own prophet to go unpunished. God would deal with the old prophet privately since his sin was a private one and was not publicly proclaimed.

Chapter 11

1. Sin changed Lucifer's appearance into something ugly; sin changed the serpent's appearance into something ugly by comparison to its original appearance. Sin causes the unsaved person to become ugly and repulsive to God.

2. God told the serpent that it would eat dust for the rest of its life. Because the serpent crawls on its belly, it does eat a certain amount of dust. But even more interesting is that in Isaiah 65:25 we are told that when God rules the world, the serpent will eat only dust.

3. We can only wonder why Satan did not enter another animal instead of the serpent. It is interesting to consider that of all the animals used as sacrifices to God, no one has ever sacrificed a serpent or any reptile to God because they are unclean according to Mosaic law. However, many pagan faiths venerate serpents.

Chapter 14

1. For instance, W.T. Purkiser, in *Exploring Our Christian Faith* (Kansas City: Beacon Hill Press, 1960), p. 218, states: "While man shares spirit with God, he shares soul with the animals."

2. H. Orton Wiley, commenting on the Genesis creation account in *Christian Theology* (Kansas City: Beacon Hill Press, 1953), p. 452, notes, "The term soul (*nephesh*) in Hebrew psychology is not peculiar to man, but represents the principle of life and sensibility in any animal organism."

SOURCES

The Amplified Bible. Grand Rapids: Zondervan, 1987.

Arnetta, Frances. "Animal Rights: A Biblical View," brochure by Christians Helping Animals and People, Inc.

Arnetta, Frances. "Questions Christians (and others) Should Ask About Animals ... And Some Answers," brochure by Christians Helping Animals and People, Inc.

Berry, George Ricker. *Greek to English Interlinear New Testament King James Version.* Iowa Falls: World Bible Publishers, 2000.

Begley, Sharon. "What Is Your Pet Thinking?" *The Wall Street Journal,* October 27, 2006, eastern edition, p. W1.

Cargal, Timothy B., Chavalas, Mark W., Edwards, James R., Gooch, John O., Handy, Lowell K., Keener, Craig S., Landry, David T. et al., eds. *The Life and Times Historical Reference Bible.* Nashville: Thomas Nelson Publishers, 1997.

CNN. Life Album. "Dogs are smarter than people think." www.CNN.com, July 2002.

Cowley, Geoffrey. "The Wisdom of Animals." *Newsweek,* May 23, 1988.

Diamond, Jared. "The Shape of Africa." *National Geographic,* September 2005.

Dunbar, Ian. *Dog Behavior: Why Dogs Do What They Do.* Neptune: T.F.H.Publishers, 1979.

Fox, Michael W. "Animals Can't Think? Think Again." *McCall's,* March 1984.

Graf, Stephenson. "All In The Family." *Science Digest,* November 1983.

Ham, Ken, Sarfati, Jonathan, Wieland, Carl. *Answers to the 4 Big Questions!.* Edited by Don Batten. USA: Answers In Genesis Ministries, 2000.

Honore, Erika K. & Klopfer, Peter H. *A Concise Survey of Animal Behavior.* New York: Academic Press Inc., 1990.

Johsson, Patrik. "New Research Opens a Window on the Minds of Plants." *Christian Science Monitor,* March 3, 2005.

Keller, Werner. *The Bible as History.* New York: William Morrow and Co. Inc., 1981.

Linden, Eugene. *The Parrot's Lament.* New York: Penguin Group, 1999.

Lindsell, Harold, ed. *Harper Study Bible; The Holy Bible.* Grand Rapids: Zondervan, 1965.

Linzey, Andrew. *Christianity and the Rights of Animals.* New York: Crossroad Publishing Company, 1987.

Marshall, I. Howard, Millard, A.R., Packer, J.I., and Wiseman, D.J., eds. *New Bible Dictionary.* Downers Grove: InterVarsity Press, 1999.

Milner, Richard. "Crabs: A Landmark Study." *Natural History*, April 2001.

"Minds of Their Own: Animals are Smarter Than You Think." *National Geographic*, March 2008.

Nave, Orville J. *Nave's Topical Bible.* Chicago: Moody Press, 1974.

Nitecki, Matthew H., and Kitchell, Jennifer A. *Evolution of Animal Behavior: Paleontological and Field Approaches.* New York: Oxford University Press, 1986.

Overall, Karen, L. *Clinical Behavioral Medicine for Small Animals.* St.Louis: Mosby, 1997.

Rifkin, Jeremy. "A Change of Heart." *Los Angeles Times,* September 1, 2003.

Rose, Kenneth Jon. "How Animals Think." *Science Digest*, February 1984.

Ryrie, Charles Caldwell. *Ryrie Study Bible.* Chicgo: Moody Press, 1995.

Sheler, Jeffery L. "Is The Bible True?" *Readers Digest*, June 2000.

Strong, James. *The New Strong's Concordance of the Bible.* Nashville: Thomas Nelson Publishers, 1985.

Time Magazine. "Birds May Do It, Bees May Do It." May 2, 1983.

Vila, Caries; Savolainen, Peter; Maldonado, Jesus E.; Amorim, Isabel R.; Rice, John E.; Honeycutt, Rodney L.; Crandall, Keith A.; Lundeberg, Joakim; Wayne, Robert K. "Multiple and Ancient Origins of the Domestic Dog." Internet paper, August 22, 2000.

Vine, W.E. *Vine's Expository Dictionary of Old and New Testament Words.* Nashville: Thomas Nelson Publishers, 1997.

Walvoord, John F. and Zuck, Roy B., eds. *The Bible Knowledge Commentary: An Exposition of the Scriptures by Dallas Seminary Faculty.* Old Testament edition. USA: Victor Books, 1988.

Weidensaul, Scott. "Tracking America's First Dog." *Smithsonian*, March 1999.

Weiskrantz, L. *Animal Intelligence.* New York: Oxford University Press, 1985.

Wheeler, John A. "The Millenium Series: Asking Infinite Questions." *National Geographic*, October 1999.

Whitney, Leon F. *Dog Psychology: The Basis of Dog Training.* New York: Howell Book House, 1976.

Zimmer, Carl. "Time in the Animal Mind." *New York Times* internet version, April 3, 2007.

ACKNOWLEDGMENTS

My greatest debt is to my family. Being raised in a supportive Christian home nurtured in me the desire to learn about God and read his Word.

My church family has also been supportive of my many questions, especially Rev. Raymond Leslie, my pastor at Colebrookdale Chapel, Boyerton, PA. I also want to thank Wimke Coltart for taking the time to read through this manuscript twice, and for giving me the encouragement that I needed. Special thanks are owed to Rufus Harvey and Brad Reinhart for their kindness in giving me computer support; like every good computer, mine did not cooperate fully while I was writing this book. I also want to thank Ruth Graybill, a wonderful missionary, who edited this manuscript for typos and grammatical errors, as well as Vi Shaffer, who reviewed it for continuity and accuracy.

I owe very special thanks to Reverend George Siebold of Open Door Church of Farmingdale, NJ, and Reverend Emmet Murphy, Executive Vice President of Roanoke Bible College, for taking the time to check my manuscript for theological accuracy.

A special thanks to Catherine Lawton, my publisher and Hannah Lawton, my editor at Cladach Publishing, for believing in me and in this manuscript.

And last but not least, I want to thank every one of my clients who expressed a sincere interest in reading this book when it became available. It was their enthusiasm that erased any doubts that I had about the need for a book of this nature.

To order additional copies of this book, contact your local
bookstore or visit the publisher's Web site at:
www.CLADACH.com
To learn about the author and her work with animals visit:
www.sbulanda.com